The Small-Game and Varmint Hunter's Bible

The Small-Game and Varmint Hunter's Bible

H. Lea Lawrence

DOUBLEDAY
NEW YORK LONDON TORONTO SYDNEY AUCKLAND

PUBLISHED BY DOUBLEDAY
a division of Bantam Doubleday Dell Publishing Group, Inc.
1540 Broadway, New York, New York 10036

DOUBLEDAY and the portrayal of an anchor with a dolphin
are registered trademarks of Doubleday, a division of Bantam
Doubleday Dell Publishing Group, Inc.

Library of Congress Cataloging-in-Publication Data

Lawrence, H. Lea, 1930–
    The Small-Game and Varmint Hunter's
        bible / H. Lea Lawrence.
        p.   cm.
    ISBN 0-385-46836-9
    1. Small-game hunting—United States.
    2. Varmint hunting—United States.
    I. Title.
    SK41.L38   1994
    799. 2'5'0973--dc20   94-1637
                                                  CIP

September 1994

10   9   8   7   6   5   4   3   2   1

First Edition

This book is dedicated to my sons,
David and Charles, who are special individuals and
excellent outdoorsmen.

ACKNOWLEDGMENTS

I wish to thank Rick Masters for his advice on both technical and general matters; Aubrey Watson, an astute professional whose personal interest in the project helped him create an array of photographs of exceptional quality; the state and federal agencies for the loan of photographs; and the many friends and contacts in the shooting and hunting industry who supplied materials and illustrations vital to the creation of the book.

Contents

Introduction

The tradition of small-game hunting in America dates back to 1620 when the first Pilgrims stepped ashore at Plymouth Rock. Having accomplished their goal of reaching a sanctuary in the New World, the matter of providing food and shelter for the colony was of principal importance. Resources for both needs were present. Raw materials for the construction of buildings—wood, stone, sand and clay—were plentiful in the region, and there was an abundance of game in the fields and forests.

For two particular reasons, small game became the main source of the meat consumed by the inhabitants of Plymouth. First, it was readily available in great quantities, and second, it was what could be most easily harvested with the somewhat primitive weapons they possessed. Their blunderbusses—muskets with flaring muzzles—were designed to throw charges of pellets just as modern shotguns do. The difference was that there was no constriction in the barrels to concentrate the charge, so they could truly be called "scatterguns." More than 200 years would pass before a choke system was devised.

Despite this handicap, the guns had a range of up to forty yards, and they were quite adequate for all kinds of small game. The rifles of that period, on the other hand, were mostly matchlocks of poor quality, because the monarchy from which the settlers had fled didn't want efficient firearms in the hands of the general public. The performance of their rifles left much to be desired, and it wasn't until after 1700 that there was much improvement. That was when the first German settlers arrived and began to manufacture the truly fine and accurate Pennsylvania long rifles that were to gain lasting fame. These muzzleloaders set a new standard for all blackpowder guns that were to follow.

The greatest advantage of the Pennsylvania rifles was that they could be produced in a variety of calibers built specifically for an intended purpose. The guns of the earlier years were mostly big-bore weapons designed mainly for killing people. They were cumbersome and virtually useless for all but large animals. Tales of early hunters "barking" squirrels—stunning them by hitting the limb on which they were sitting—are true, but it wasn't to demonstrate their marksmanship. They did it because the

The Pennsylvania long rifle was a great improvement over the blunderbusses of the earliest settlers. A muzzleloader with a flintlock action, it was the first reliable and accurate gun on the American frontier.

big bullets would blow a squirrel to pieces. Once the squirrel was knocked out of the tree and on the ground, it could be fully dispatched.

The light, graceful Pennsylvania rifles with smaller bores were much better suited for squirrels, rabbits and similar kinds of game. They were remarkably accurate, and they quickly became the favorites of hunters. It was a point of pride to be a skillful marksman, and shooting matches were a popular form of entertainment among the frontiersmen.

As more settlers arrived from England and Europe, and the westward movement continued, small game remained an important part of the pioneers' diet while on the move. Hunters were assigned to forage for game as they traveled. Even when their goals were reached and homesteads created, small game continued to be the most important source of meat. Cows were for milk, poultry primarily for eggs and down, sheep for wool, and swine were often sold or bartered rather than slaughtered for food. Besides, in most areas small game seemed limitless and was easy to harvest.

Meanwhile, in the East, civilization was firmly taking hold as more families put down permanent roots. The population was mostly rural, and farms were producing ever-increasing amounts of food. Still, though small game was no longer essential for survival, it remained a substantial and desirable dietary supplement.

In many cases, the responsibility for collecting squirrels and rabbits was delegated to youngsters. This was hardly an unpleasant assignment, being fun rather than a chore. Most young hunters cut their teeth on small game, and this was the basis for a tradition that remains dominant. Small-game hunting continues to be the most popular of all of the shooting sports.

The distinction between small game and varmints often differs from state to state according to how they are classified by game departments. A maze of regulations governs hunting methods and seasons. Because of the volume and complexity of these myriad differences in the regulations, it would be impossible, or at least impractical, to list them. Since the status of certain birds and animals changes from year to year, the information would soon be dated. The best solution is to check the laws of the state where you plan to hunt.

Varmints offer the hunter extra shooting opportunity of an exciting sort, both during and in between the regular seasons. Traditionally, varmints have been regarded as incidental to mainstream hunting except by a relatively small group of dedicated shooters. However, in recent years this has changed. Varminting has become very popular, and there are many hunters who find it the most challenging and satisfying of all pursuits available in the field.

The sport offers special advantages, one of which is that many of the creatures included in this category are unprotected. They can be sought anytime of the year. Another is that competition for these species is markedly less than for game birds and animals. Also, because there are so many different kinds of varmints throughout North America, there's opportunity almost everywhere.

Varmints have a long history in this country. While small game was indeed a blessing for the early settlers, it didn't take long for them to discover wildlife species that were detrimental to their daily lives in one way or another. Along with the good came the bad.

The problems became apparent once the colonists prepared ground for the first planting. From the time fields were sown right on through harvest time, crops were plagued by

various kinds of marauders. As soon as seeds were placed in the ground, crows and other birds plucked them out. When the first sprouts pushed up through the earth, woodchucks began feasting on the bounty. And throughout the entire growing season, farmers fought a constant battle with vandals of one kind or another.

Yet crops weren't the only targets. Domestic fowl were always in danger from foxes, weasels, bobcats and hawks. The young of some domestic livestock also fell victim to the larger predators.

The best defense—or offense—against these damaging creatures was the gun, so just as the tradition of hunting small game began at the Plymouth Colony, so did the tradition of varmint hunting.

At the outset it wasn't viewed as a sport. Rather, it was an almost everyday task necessary for the protection of crops, livestock and, in some instances, human beings. The goal was to eradicate the offenders, or at least to eliminate as many as possible.

These predatory species were called by many names: *vermin, pirates, brigands, ravishers, thieves* and *looters*, and no doubt some profane ones, as well. Some of these may still be in use, but today "varmint" is the most common term for the "bad guys."

Over the years some predators that once economically impacted crops and livestock have been reduced in numbers to the point they no longer remain significant threats. In some instances wildlife agencies manage these varmints to achieve a reasonable balance and to avoid overkill. Other species once branded as detrimental, such as hawks, owls and eagles, have been placed on the protected list almost everywhere. Even some of the reptiles now fall into the protected category, and in some cases even poisonous species can't be killed. Snapping turtles still offer opportunity in most places, and plinking them with a .22 can be a great asset to a lake or pond where waterfowl or shorebirds nest, since these creatures are effective predators. They devour young birds, and are able to maim or cripple adults.

Even with such exceptions, there's no shortage of varmints that can be hunted. Throughout the continent all kinds of opportunities exist, and at some locations, a veritable potpourri of choices is offered. Alaska is a good example, where bats, shrews, rats, mice, porcupines, raccoons, lynx, starlings, cormorants, crows, foxes and coyotes can be hunted in all or some of the twenty-six units, some with no season or bag limits. In most places virtually all of the rodents are unprotected, as are a few birds, although crows are the only ones that get serious attention.

There have been changes in the ways in which animals and birds, game or varmints, can be taken. Once, any type of motorized vehicles, including boats, were legal, as were airplanes and helicopters. There are now various federal and state laws that strictly govern all of these things. One, The Airborne Hunting Act of 1956 (and subsequent amendments in 1971 and 1972) prohibits the use of any type of aircraft for hunting or harassing any fish, birds or

animals. The only exceptions are in cases where predation permits are issued to landowners suffering damage or authorized federal or state game and fish agencies. As for game birds and animals other than migratory waterfowl, there are many places where vehicles can be used, but in each case there are specific rules that apply regarding the how's, where's and when's.

Yet even though restrictions have been placed on many birds and animals for good reason, those that have been the main interest of varmint hunters over the years—woodchucks, prairie dogs, crows, coyotes, bobcats and others—have been little affected. They're still highly prolific; and farmers, ranchers and landowners want them eliminated or reduced in numbers. Hence varmint shooters often gain access to places denied other hunters. Since most wildlife agencies agree that this is the best way to control or manage a varmint population, everybody's happy. Looking ahead, there are good reasons to believe that this sport is going to remain popular and will supplement the lost opportunities in hunting game animals.

Gray Squirrel

1

Squirrels

Sometimes scientific, or taxonomic, names are poetic and sometimes they are specific. However, in the instance of Sciuridae, the squirrel family, neither seems to apply. In Latin, this means "shade-tail," referring to the habit some of the species exhibit of holding a bushy tail over their backs. Since most of the animals in this category have short, slim tails that would produce a very little shade, the Latin name is not very accurate.

Distributed from Mexico to the Arctic, the squirrel family is large and diverse. It consists of sixty-three species, ranging in size from tiny chipmunks that weigh less than 2 ounces to large hoary marmots that may attain 20 pounds.

Of these sixty-three species, only three that are classified as tree squirrels are of major importance to small-game hunters. It's a much different situation where varmint hunters are concerned, but that will be discussed later.

Of this trio of true shade-tails, the one most familiar to hunters, as well as to the general public, is the **Gray Squirrel**. These highly popular game animals are generally present wherever

nut trees are found, whether it be in large hardwood stands or small woodlots. They're also equally at home in urban settings, and few city parks and suburban neighborhoods within their extensive range are without them.

Squirrels and nuts are synonymous. Acorns are the most abundant mast crop throughout their range, but squirrels also feed on hickory nuts, walnuts, pecans and beechnuts. They bury nuts, but despite common belief, they don't recall the locations. However, they are able to smell them, even through snow cover, so they retrieve many at times when food is most vital. Yet while mast is a mainstay during the fall and winter months, their overall menu includes many other items. They eat maple, tulip and pine tree seeds, fruit, mushrooms and other fungi, flowers and young buds. In agricultural areas, they often ravish corn fields from the time the ears first appear until harvest time.

In some locations hunters refer to grays as cat squirrels, probably because of the mewing sounds they sometimes make. Another possible reason is their quick, darting, catlike movements.

Gray squirrels occupy cavities in trees in the

winter, usually natural openings caused by disease or fire, or holes made by woodpeckers.
These dens are lined with leaves and provide
snug quarters during harsh weather. In extreme
conditions, squirrels may remain in their dens
for up to several days, but unlike some other
rodents they don't hibernate, staying active
throughout the winter. In the summer they
build leaf nests that are perched in crotches or
in forks of limbs. Some of these are ball shaped
and well constructed, with living space inside;
others are flimsy, flat structures used mainly as
platforms for sunning or loafing.

The major feeding activity takes place in early
morning and late afternoon, yet sometimes all
day if food is scarce. Though seldom observed,
they often feed on tender tree buds on moonlit
nights in the springtime. In times of overpopu-
lation or mast failures, mass migrations may
occur as a survival attempt.

Although this species is usually quite uniform
in color, with gray above and white underparts,
there is a black phase common to parts of its
northern range. There are also scattered colonies
of albino gray squirrels, most of which are found
in towns or cities where they are protected.
Adults weigh between 14 and 25 ounces.

Of all the tree squirrels, gray squirrels have
the largest range. They're found in all of the
eastern states, in Iowa, the eastern parts of
North Dakota, Southern Manitoba, Oklahoma,
Kansas and Texas.

The **Fox Squirrel** is a larger, less graceful animal than the gray, and throughout its range
there are several distinct color phases. In the
North it is yellowish-brown on the upperparts,
and yellow to orange underneath; in the South
it is grayish-grizzled above, whitish below, with
a dark head and white nose. Other variations
include specimens that are all black except for
white-tipped nose and ears, and others that are
steel blue. Weights vary according to locations,
and usually average about 2 pounds in adults.
However, specimens of over 3 pounds do occur.

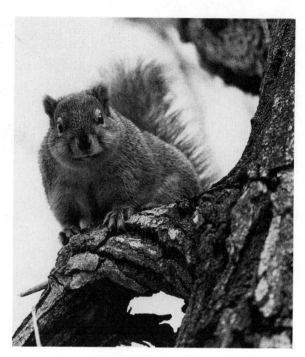

Fox Squirrel

This species occupies a broad spectrum of
habitat types: oak-hickory hardwood stands,
cypress and mangrove swamps, live oaks and
mixed forests, and piney woods.

Fox squirrels have an appetite for almost anything they can find. All kinds of nuts, berries,
seeds, bulbs, fruit, roots, insects, bird eggs,
fungi, buds and the inner bark of maple trees
are relished. Like their cousins, they also will
wreak havoc on corn fields. When foraging,
they ordinarily travel considerable distances
from their dens, usually moving along on the
ground rather than through the trees. Also, seeing one in an open field isn't uncommon.

This species also occupies leaf nests in the
summer, but these are nearly always nestled in
the crotches of trees instead of on upper or outer
limbs. Because of their larger body size and
weight, they need such perches for greater stability. When resting or loafing, they stretch out on
broad limbs and use their tail as a parasol, living
up to their family name. In the winter, holes or
cavities that afford plenty of space are preferred,

The Delmarva fox squirrel is one of several subspecies.

since several animals may share dens during this period. In places where both fox and gray squirrels are present, there's little contact between the species, although it's likely they compete for den space when winter approaches.

Fox squirrels are early risers, popping out of their nests or dens at first light and bounding out through the woods to dine on whatever they can find. With the need for a greater amount of food than gray squirrels, they go about this activity with zest, and usually for a longer period. Once satisfied, they either begin roaming or retire for an after-breakfast nap.

Extensive hardwood clearing in the Northeast has reduced fox squirrel numbers; and their presence has been eliminated in the New England states, most of New Jersey and parts of New York and Pennsylvania. Otherwise, they're found throughout the East and west to the Dakotas, northeastern Colorado and eastern Texas.

The **Western Gray Squirrel** bears a close resemblance to its eastern relatives except that it has numerous white-tipped hairs on the upperparts that give it a more silvery appearance, and the backs of the ears are reddish-brown. The weight range is between 12 and 34 ounces.

These squirrels are found mainly in the redwood and hardwood forests common to the range they occupy. They build nests of shredded bark and leaves high above the ground for summer occupancy and spend the winter in tree hollows, cavities or woodpecker holes.

Their habits are similar to the other two major tree squirrels. Chief foods are acorns, pine nuts, fungi, fruits, berries, bird eggs and insects. This squirrel possesses a keen sense of smell and a superior memory that allows it to recover the majority of the nuts it buries.

This is the only squirrel in the West that's eagerly sought by hunters, and its range extends all the way from Washington to California. The areas of greatest abundance are the large forested areas in the coastal and inland mountain ranges.

Within the remaining tree-squirrel varieties, only one is hunted for food, while the rest are seldom, if ever, pursued for this purpose. One species is extremely low in numbers.

Abert's Squirrel, also known as the tassel-eared squirrel, is a brightly-colored animal similar in size to the gray. It has dark gray upperparts accented with black and russet, and white underparts. Its trademark is its tufted ears. This species inhabits conifer forests and depends upon pine seeds and pinon nuts as its principal foods, but it also eats other items such as dropped antlers, fungi, berries and weedy plants. It builds nests in tree crotches and lines them with shredded bark.

The range of the Abert's squirrel is in the isolated mountains of Arizona, southeast Utah, Colorado and New Mexico. A subspecies, the **Kaibab Squirrel**, is found only on the North Rim of the Grand Canyon and is considered endangered.

The **Red Squirrel**, sometimes called the *pine squirrel* or *chickaree*, is small, with reddish to grayish back and sides and whitish underparts. It occupies coniferous, hardwood, and mixed forests. Pine seeds are a major diet item, but it also will eat all of the other foods typical in tree squirrel menus. The range is broad, extending from the tree limit in the North and through-

out most of Alaska and Canada; both the Rocky Mountain and Appalachian regions; the northeastern states; and Ohio, Indiana, Michigan, Illinois, Iowa, Minnesota and Wisconsin.

Call the **Douglas Squirrel** a virtual twin of the red squirrel, since its nicknames are the same, as are its habits. One difference is that it's a very noisy animal with a wide variety of calls that are often an annoyance to hunters who are stalking other game. It is found in southwestern British Columbia, the western parts of Washington and Oregon, and western California.

The **Southern Flying Squirrel** has a silky fur that is grayish-brown above and white below, with large black eyes. Strictly nocturnal, these timid creatures occupy hardwood forests and prefer holes in trees as nests, although they sometimes build summer nests of leaves. Despite their name, they glide rather than fly. Berries, nuts, fungi and insects are the main elements of their diet.

The range includes all of the eastern states

Red Squirrel

except New England and the lower portion of Florida; west to Minnesota and the eastern parts of Kansas and Texas.

The **Northern Flying Squirrel** is dark brown above and white below, and its habits are nearly identical to the southern variety. Its range is more broad, however, extending all across Canada and into Alaska; in California, Idaho, Utah, Montana and Wyoming; eastward through the northern states to New England; and into the Appalachians.

HUNTING METHODS

Lessons learned in squirrel hunting can be the most valuable training any hunter, young or

There's no better way for a youngster to learn squirrel hunting than with a father or other experienced adult.

old, can acquire. The things necessary for success include all of the elements required for seeking virtually any other small- or big-game species, which gave rise to the statement that "a good squirrel hunter can hunt anything."

Over the years millions of hunters have cut their teeth on squirrels. For a youngster, there's no better way to get started, especially if he or she is lucky enough to have a father or some other experienced person along as a teacher. It's impossible to forget the magic of the first squirrel hunt and the spine-tingling thrill of being in the woods in the spooky, predawn atmosphere. It's a feeling that persists, no matter how many times the experience is repeated.

Squirrels are very wary creatures. A hunter must be able to move through the woods silently, or Indian style. It isn't as easy as it might seem, since there are times when it is next to impossible to proceed noiselessly. Walking in dry leaves is the ultimate challenge, and those familiar with this situation know that it's as delicate an operation as balancing on a tightrope. The keys are patience and an ability to move very slowly and deliberately, picking out each spot where a foot is going to be placed with great caution. All movements must be in slow motion. A quick turn of the head or a hand swatting away an insect are all it takes to bring a stalk to an instantaneous end, regardless of how well one has performed otherwise. Stalking can be at once both the most difficult and most satisfying aspects of the sport, because succeeding means that you've outwitted one of the most sound-conscious creatures in the wild.

But there's more to squirrel hunting than just stealth. Squirrels have eyesight quite as keen as their hearing. Besides moving silently, a hunter must remain as invisible as possible.

Squirrels make noises, too. In the dim light of early morning, these sounds are the only clues to their whereabouts. It's important to be able to distinguish squirrel sounds from other forest noises.

One thing that definitely signals *squirrel* is

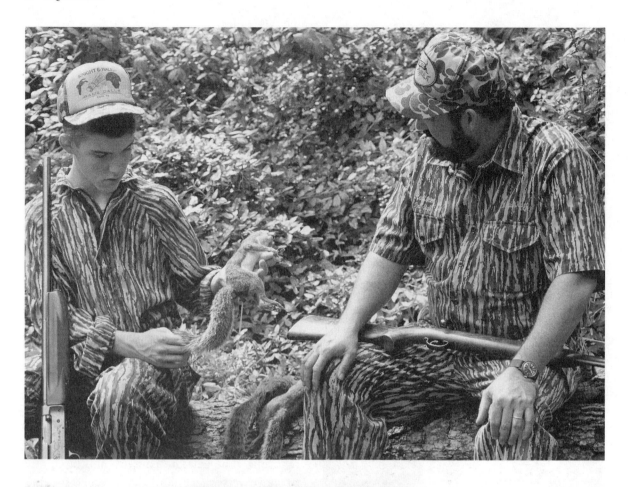

A youth looks over his first squirrel taken on a hunt with his father.

Patience is one of the prime factors in becoming a successful squirrel hunter. Sitting quietly near mast trees almost always pays off.

It's fairly easy to move up on squirrels when they're cutting nuts, because the noise they make obliterates other sounds.

the "whooshing" sound they make when leaping from tree to tree. When they're in motion, they aren't likely to detect other noises, so it's an ideal time to move and gain a little ground in the direction from which the sound comes. Often squirrels congregate on a particular feeding spot, which may be a single hickory or oak, and getting close and in position can be the key to success.

Even if you can't get within range of the feed-

ing location immediately, all you have to do is wait until the animals begin cutting nuts. This is another activity that muffles their ability to hear other sounds. The clatter of hulls and shells falling sounds like rain in the forest, and they make additional noises as they dash back and forth gathering more nuts. The more squirrels that are in the tree, the greater the din becomes.

If there's sufficient light, spotting the early movement in the trees is easy, but there's a trick to visually covering a broad expanse of woods. The idea is not to focus on any particular spot. Instead, look straight ahead without any object in mind and let your eyes function like a wide-angle camera lens, taking advantage of your peripheral vision. This way you pick up every flicker of motion in a full 180-degree field of view.

How close you need to approach your quarry depends on what kind of shooting equipment you're using. A hunter with a .22 caliber rimfire rifle, particularly if scope-sighted, can pick off squirrels much farther away than a person using a shotgun. The latter has a maximum dependable killing range of less than fifty yards, while the rifle can be effective up to more than twice that distance. Usually, though, hunters prefer to get in as close as possible, partly so they can be surer of their shots, but also because of the satisfaction in conducting a good stalk.

When woods are very dry, sitting is the most productive method. If you know the area, you'll be aware of where squirrels are feeding. Go to the spot before daylight and get yourself situated. Pick out a spot and clear the area around where you plan to sit of all leaves and twigs so any movement you make won't create noise. With this tactic, you're waiting for the squirrels to come to you instead of going to them.

One of the most enjoyable ways to hunt bushytails is to float down a stream in a tube. This is a truly *silent* approach, and one which permits you to cover a lot of territory in a single outing. Some hunters using this tactic combine hunting squirrels with fishing, a form of the sport

Canoes and flat-bottomed aluminum boats are ideal for float hunting for squirrels and provide a stable shooting platform.

The float tube provides an excellent way to hunt on smaller streams where boats aren't able to navigate in the shallows.

that is also very conducive to overnight trips. Drifting along quietly on a bright October day is exhilarating in itself, and when you can combine it with shooting squirrels, it's even better!

Canoes or flat-bottomed aluminum boats also are ideal for this kind of hunting, which can be done either solo or with a partner. It's much more practical with two, since one person can handle the craft while the other keeps an eye out for action. The usual rule is one shot apiece between swapping roles.

Almost every state has waters that are suitable for this hunting technique, and topographical maps can help locate them. Picking stretches that pass through forested areas is best, but even those that have bordering strips of woods can be

winners. Squirrels like to be close to water, and often they will occupy the trees that line the banks, particularly if those trees are mast-bearing. Too, stream and river bottomlands have plenty of the other foods squirrels eat throughout the year.

There's another kind of "bushytail boulevard" that's overlooked by most hunters, yet it's one that provides special advantages which can pay big dividends throughout the season. Also, it's an ace in the hole that can sometimes save the day when other approaches fail.

What's the secret? Railroad tracks.

And the next question: why?

Think about it for a minute. Railroad tracks that pass through forested areas provide a way to walk through the woods silently and with a minimum of effort. When drought conditions exist and the leaves are tinder dry, it's impossible to move quietly in the woods, regardless of how carefully you proceed. Walking along the tracks, however, allows you to be virtually silent. Then if squirrel activity is detected, you can proceed without having to attempt a lengthy and often futile stalk.

That's an example of an extreme situation, but using the rail route is a very productive and enjoyable way to hunt no matter what conditions prevail. There are many benefits other than being able to stalk noiselessly. Another is that a lot of territory can be covered, increasing the odds for success. Sometimes tall trees along each side of the track overlap above it and create leafy bridges on which squirrels pass back and forth. This shooting opportunity, combined with the action hunters usually find directly adjacent to the tracks, can result in a limit of bushytails being bagged without ever stepping off the roadbed.

Locating woodlands through which railroads pass isn't difficult, and a look at a topographic map of your area will probably disclose several that are worth investigating. And don't concentrate only on lines currently in use. There are many abandoned routes that may offer even better potential.

Scouting the woods and locating feeding sites in advance is always a smart strategy. Then you can get into position before daylight. According to the part of the country you're in and what kind of trees are found, identifying those to which squirrels are attracted at different times of the season is a big help. For instance, in the forests of the East, beech may be the first mast,

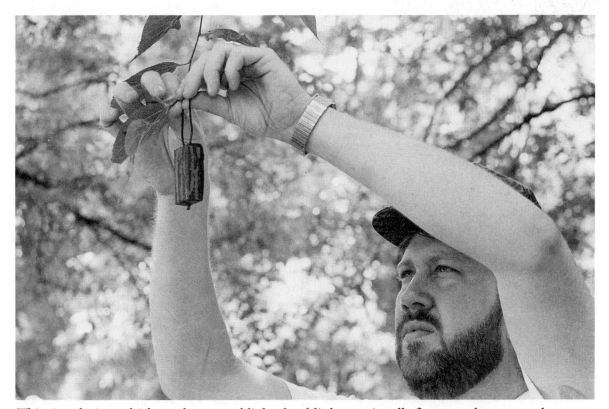

This tiny device, which produces a red light that blinks continually for more than a month on one battery, can be hung on a limb to assist a hunter in locating his stand before daylight.

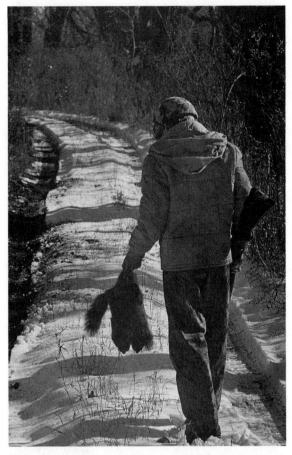

Squirrels tend to remain inactive during severe storms or bad weather, but catching them out on the first sunny day can result in a nice bag.

followed by white oak and hickory. Next will be the various other kinds of oak and black walnut. At times when mast crops are meager, squirrels will cut pine cones, the fruit of osage orange and many seed-producing trees and shrubs which are normally low on the preference list. Don't forget that if there's a cornfield near the woods, this is also a prime spot for squirrels. Squirrels like corn at any stage of development, and in the fall when the crop is mature and ready for harvest, they usually pay daily visits to the fields. Generally this activity takes place between mid-morning and mid-afternoon, the times when they're most likely to be foraging on the ground. Finding fresh cut-

tings of any of these items is a clue to where squirrels are active.

Though squirrels normally feed in early morning and late afternoon, as winter approaches they're liable to be foraging through the woods at any time of the day. Once the foliage is gone, most of this travel will be on the ground. In damp woods they're as silent as ghosts, and it takes a sharp eye to catch their movements.

Weather is an important factor. Squirrels are most active on calm days, whether sunny or cloudy. On windy days they are less active; they don't like conditions that interfere with their ability to sense danger. Light rain usually isn't a deterrent, and it's great for a stalking hunter. During severe weather, squirrels will remain in their dens, often for days at a time.

Once the leaves are off the trees, stalking becomes even more difficult, since squirrels have exceedingly sharp eyesight. A scope-sighted .22 rifle has a big advantage over a shotgun, because long shots are the rule rather than the exception. This kind of shooting is an excellent test of a hunter's marksmanship. Serious hunters make certain they can hit what they shoot at, and accuracy is a part of a hunter's responsibility. A little practice on a range during the off seasons can go a long way in keeping this skill well-honed.

Hunters sometimes see squirrels run into the leaf nests they build for summer occupancy, but the temptation to shoot into these should be avoided. It's an unethical practice, because the nests may still contain young. Too, even if only one animal is present, there's a good chance it may die inside the nest and cannot be recovered. There's nothing wrong with throwing rocks or sticks at the nest in an effort to flush the animal out, and some hunters carry a slingshot with which to lob rocks farther and more accurately. The idea isn't to penetrate the nest, only to use enough power to hit it or the tree limb beside it and put the squirrel on the run. If this can't be accomplished, the other options are to sit and wait for the squirrel to emerge, or move on and hope to find success elsewhere.

Hunters should also avoid shooting at a squirrel with its head protruding from a hole in a tree. If shot, it will almost always fall back into the cavity, and no hunter wants to lose game in this manner.

Two special aids that enhance your chances of success can be of value in both early and late season situations.

One is the use of a squirrel dog to locate the animals and keep them bayed until you arrive. Nothing beats this approach when it comes to finding plenty of animals, and it's a lot of fun to follow a dog through the woods until it sniffs

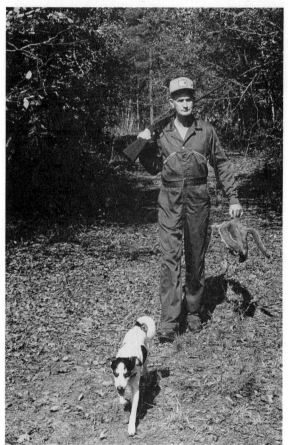

A dog can add much pleasure to the hunt, because once it spots a squirrel, chances are you'll soon have it in your bag.

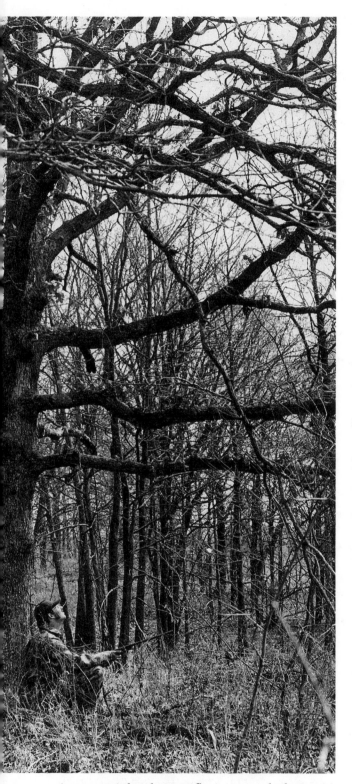

A scope-sighted .22 rifle is a good choice in winter when the trees are bare and it's very difficult to get within shotgun range.

There are many kinds of squirrel calls on the market, including reed calls and whistles; friction-type calls; and ones operated by percussion. Their effectiveness varies considerably.

out a trail or spots a bushytail and gives chase.

There's no particular way to define these dogs except to say that the instinct to hunt squirrels may occur in any breed. Small mongrel dogs, known as "feists," have always been popular, and while their ancestry may be varied and complex, it is likely that a good dose of terrier is somewhere in the lineage. Feists don't have the territory all to themselves, because the instinct to go after squirrels can show up in a broad variety of canines of all shapes, sizes and blood lines.

There's a problem, however, in finding a squirrel dog. This wasn't the case when America was mostly rural, since every farm boy had what could best be called an all-purpose dog that

would go after almost anything. All a hunter had to do to locate one was ask around at a country store. Usually someone would know of a youngster who'd be happy to act as guide and dog handler for a box of cartridges or a fifty-cent piece. Today, very few squirrel dogs exist, and having access to one is a major coup.

The other aid—a squirrel call—is one to which everyone has easy access. Nearly every sporting goods store and hunting catalog features one or several models.

There's by no means a universal acceptance of these devices, and with good reason. Most are of little value except to entertain the hunter and give him the false hope of possessing a secret weapon.

Also, the term *call* is somewhat misleading, since in almost every case the most that can be expected is to attract attention or get a reply. Squirrel language isn't well understood, but there's wide agreement that they do communicate vocally. The scolding sounds they make when angry or alarmed are easy to comprehend, but those who have listened carefully and extensively to "squirrel talk" know they make a variety of sounds, some of which are very subtle and can be heard only at very close range.

There are two effective calls. One is a call with an accordion-type rubber attachment that you tap to supply air to a double reed system that operates on both expulsion and intake. With a little prac-tice, you can produce sounds that are remarkably authentic—chatters, barks and squeals—to which squirrels often readily respond.

The other is a whistle call that mimics the sound made by a young squirrel under attack by a predator. This triggers the maternal and pater-nal instincts in adult squirrels, and they expose themselves and begin scolding in protest. To make the scene more realistic, the hunter bends over a small sapling and swats the ground with its leafy top while calling. This is intended to represent the flailing of hawk or owl wings as they subdue their prey.

Almost all squirrel seasons are set in the fall and winter months, but there are four states

This hunter took a nice bag of gray squirrels with a whistle call that imitates the sound of a young squirrel in distress.

A few states have spring squirrel seasons. Mulberries are one of the prime foods the animals seek at this time.

that offer spring opportunity: Missouri, Arkansas, Texas and Oklahoma. This is traditional in these states, and called "mulberry seasons" in some places because of the squirrels' fondness for this fruit. They also feed heavily on the buds of some young trees, emerging fungi and other new growth. Wildlife officials claim that this early season has no adverse effect on the squirrel population. These animals, like many other rodents, don't have a spring, or one-time, mating period. They reproduce throughout the year, and young may be present in the nests at any time.

EQUIPMENT AND ACCESSORIES

The .22 rimfire rifle and the .410 shotgun are the most popular guns for squirrel hunting, and while it's rare that rifle calibers larger than .22 are employed except by blackpowder enthusiasts who prefer .32 caliber, it's not uncommon for hunters to use shotguns in 20, 16 and 12 gauge. The sport has a following of handgunners, and again, the .22 rimfire is the favorite choice.

There's a choice between long rifle, long and short cartridges in both solid and hollow-point styles. Solids will pass through a squirrel without great tissue damage, but the mushrooming hol-

low point usually has devastating results. The argument against solids is that they often cripple and allow the animal to escape and hide. This is true, yet for those hunters who prefer to shoot squirrels in the head, it makes little difference. The target is fairly small, and you either score a deadly hit or miss entirely. This is where a good scope can provide a big advantage, particularly in low light conditions. Very few hunters use shorts or longs, since the long-rifle cartridges provide maximum power and performance.

If you get within shooting range of a squirrel, and have a good scope and a steady hand, it's possible to make head shots that don't destroy meat. It's a challenge, and with such a small target, there's no danger of crippling the animal; you're either going to hit or miss.

As for shotguns, No. 6 or 7½ shot is usually adequate, although some prefer No. 4s for big fox squirrels. Most important is getting within good killing distance, which varies according to shotgun gauge. The difference between the effective range of a .410 and that of a 12 gauge is as much as 20 yards. Too, the 12 gauge sends out a much larger shot charge. Most hunters prefer full-choke barrels since a tight pattern is needed for a squirrel in a tall tree.

Hunting squirrels with other kinds of

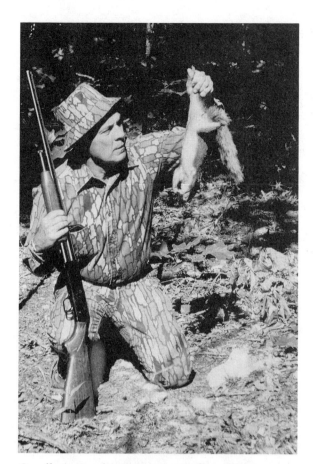

Camouflaged clothing is preferable, especially when the pattern is matched up with the colors of the woods at the time. Brushed cotton is the best fabric, because it's practically noiseless when it comes in contact with leaves or twigs. A face mask and camouflaged gloves are helpful.

Light, compact binoculars are a very useful accessory, particularly during those periods when the woods are barren of foliage. With this optical advantage, squirrel activity can be seen from a distance, allowing you to develop an approach strategy. They're useful at all times in locating squirrels that are hiding in foliage, lying outstretched on limbs, or tucked into crotches of trees.

Binoculars can bring a lot of additional pleasure to the hunt. It's fun to sit and scan the woods, watching whatever activity interests you. Those who enjoy bird watching can view them

Small-gauge shotguns are preferred by a great many hunters. They're particularly effective in early season when the foliage is still on the trees and it's easier to get into close range.

weapons also enjoys a certain amount of popularity. Blackpowder enthusiasts like to stalk them the "old-fashioned way" with muzzleloaders; handgunners go after them with .22 caliber pistols; and bowhunters find bushytails a special challenge.

Since stealth is paramount, footwear and clothing that facilitate quiet and unobtrusive movement should be chosen. Rubber-bottomed pacs are favorites of many hunters. They're soft, comfortable and lend good ankle support. Also, they're waterproof and ideal for traveling in wet and marshy spots. Moccasins and canvas walking shoes are okay, too, except in wet weather.

The single-shot .410 shotgun packs enough punch to knock down a big fox squirrel, and it's an ideal choice for beginners.

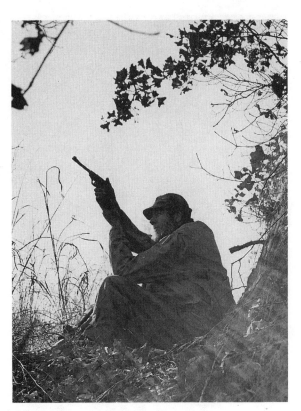

Some hunters like to go after squirrels with a muzzleloader, hunting them in the "old-fashioned" way, but a lighter, more compact modern version like this Connecticut Valley Arms squirrel rifle in .32 caliber is more practical. Hunting with a .22 caliber pistol (right) is a challenge and has numerous followers.

in their natural surroundings instead of on a feeder. Hawks ordinarily patrol woods looking for squirrels and other rodents, and in early morning there's a chance to get a look at owls before they retire for the day. And few woods are devoid of chipmunks.

A day pack or fanny pack can be very useful for carrying insect and tick repellant, flashlight, compass, waterproof match case or fire-starting kit, notebook and pencil, first-aid kit and whatever else that's needed, including snacks or a lunch.

In places where squirrel season opens while the weather is still quite warm, mosquitoes and other biting insects can often make a hunter's life miserable. This plague can be virtually assured in the southern tier of states, and it's so severe in some

Small, compact binoculars can be very helpful, since they allow squirrel activity to be spotted from a distance.

Ticks, mosquitoes and other kinds of biting insects are likely to be encountered during the early part of the squirrel season, and minor accidents can occur. It's wise to be prepared for these annoyances.

low-lying areas that hunters avoid them until later in the season. Mosquitoes can easily penetrate the light clothing worn at this time of year, so unless repellant is applied all over the body, you're going to get bitten a lot.

There's a solution, though, and it's in a mesh-like outfit worn over the hunting clothes that's permeated with potent repellant. It provides head-to-ankle protection and makes it possible to go confidently into infested areas. The outfit can be worn over and over again, and when its potency wanes, it's a simple matter to recharge it to full strength.

Sitting under trees and watching for squirrels can sometimes be quite uncomfortable, especially when the ground is wet. To avoid this, take along one of the light, camouflaged cushions that can be attached to a belt. There's also an inflatable model that can be carried in the pack.

One other thing that can come in handy is a small camera. All that's needed to justify this addition is to think of all of the times you've wished you had one!

This mesh-type suit repels insects, yet allows plenty of air flow. The suit is treated with insect repellent and can be used several times without recharging.

2

Rabbits and Hares

Rabbits and hares are the most popular small game in North America, and historically they have supplied more sport and food for the table than any other animal. This isn't surprising, considering both their enormous reproductive capabilities and the fact that there are over a dozen and a half species scattered throughout the continent from the Arctic to Central America. Of this number, all but two are native species. In the United States at least one variety can be found in every state, and in some instances there are several kinds present. In most states, rabbits and hares are considered game animals.

Except for some differences in size, weight and coloration, these animals are look-alikes, with long ears and powerful hind legs. Their diets are similar, also. They eat only vegetable matter—grasses, plants, berries, tree bark, shrubs tubers, farm grains and produce—whatever is available in their home territories. Another characteristic they share is a preference for feeding at night.

Some rabbits and hares are burrowers, others build nests above ground in dense cover such as briar patches, honeysuckle thickets, brushpiles or woody tangles. They need all the protection they can get, since they have a host of natural enemies. Coyotes, foxes, bobcats, weasels, hawks and owls prey on them, as well as house cats, dogs and, of course, man. A talent for multiplying is their only defense against extinction. It's interesting to note that they're also able to manipulate population levels with what could be called "a built-in balance system" that automatically regulates the size and frequency of litters. Food availability is the key, so when lean conditions exist, fewer young are born, and the opposite is true in good times. Sometimes food supplies become superabundant and population explosions occur that cost farmers millions of dollars in crop depredation. At such times it's often necessary to use drastic means to reduce the numbers.

Several of the species are broadly distributed, while others have restricted ranges. One variety is found only in small parts of two southwestern states where the dwindling population is subjected to very little gunning pressure. Some other types aren't important as game but are paid plenty of attention by varmint hunters.

The **Eastern Cottontail's** extensive range

Eastern Cottontail

encompasses all of the eastern United States, most of the Midwest, and parts of the Southwest, mainly Texas, New Mexico and Arizona. It's plentiful in all of these regions, and more hunters seek this species than any other small game.

This rabbit is gray-brown, sometimes with a white spot on the forehead and a rusty hue around the nape of the neck. The ears are long and the feet whitish. Body weight is generally 2 to 4 pounds. Several other rabbits share similar characteristics, and where ranges overlap this sometimes leads to confusion in identification.

During the past several decades, this cottontail has displayed a remarkable talent for adapting to the changes that have taken place within its range. The disappearance of small farms saw the passing of fencerows, fallow fields, briar patches and other features that were prime rabbit cover located in close proximity to the agri-

cultural crops that are their main food sources. The coming of large farm operations brought about the elimination of the cover, resulting in fields that are as bare as a tabletop. This meant that there were very few places of refuge adjacent to the crops upon which they depended for much of their food supply. Another factor entered into the picture: urban sprawl, which reduced suitable habitat even further. With hunting pressure constantly mounting, the cottontail was caught in a vise.

Unlike some other game animals and birds that can be managed with various kinds of manipulations, the cottontail cannot. This animal is a byproduct of agricultural practices. When the big changes in farming began taking place, rabbits had to "do or die," and they did it successfully.

The route they took to fit themselves into the

scheme of things is a study in survival against pretty steep odds. Since cover was no longer available at places adjacent to the pastures and farm crops, the rabbits sought it elsewhere. This didn't mean they abandoned their food sources. They simply found secure spots that are often as much as a mile away. They come to the feeding areas after dark and return before daylight. Today, visiting cover remote from what were once hotspots is the best way to locate cottontails.

One other adaptation should be noted. The "new rabbits" tend to be much less nervous and high-strung than their predecessors. They hold tighter and often let hunters or dogs pass within a few feet if they sense they're undetected. This adds new dimensions and added challenges to the sport.

The **New England Cottontail** is very similar in size and appearance to the Eastern Cottontail. The main distinguishing characteristic is a black spot between the ears. Woods and brushlands are the preferred habitat, and the range is limited to New England and south into the Alleghenies.

Marsh Rabbits like bottomlands, swamps, the edges of waterways and lakes. They have short ears and are dark brown above with a cinnamon-colored collar and a dark, short tail. They occupy all of Florida and lowland areas of Georgia, the Carolinas and Virginia.

The **Swamp Rabbit**, or "cane-cutter," is the largest of the rabbits, weighing up to 6 pounds. It is similar in appearance to the smaller marsh rabbit but has a thin white tail and rust-colored feet. An excellent swimmer, it takes to the water without hesitation and can remain submerged with only its nose above the surface. Swamp rabbits are found in canebrakes, bottomlands and swamps in eastern Texas and Oklahoma and eastward to southern Illinois and northern Georgia. They leave their droppings on stumps or logs and eat them again when food is scarce. This is a form of primitive recycling, but one not unknown in other parts of the animal kingdom.

Cape or European Hares are exotics that were brought into New York in the late 1800s with the idea of establishing a new game species larger than the cottontail that would promote sport hunting. They eventually spread to other parts of New England and west to the Great Lakes region. They were also released in Pennsylvania, New Jersey, Maryland, Indiana, Illinois, Wisconsin, the Farallon Islands off California, Middelm Island off Alaska, and San Juan Island off Washington. At the last location they multiplied to the point of being serious pests. Their burrows, or warrens, were causing extensive damage. Large chunks of land were falling off into the sea, and the lighthouse on the island nearly collapsed before eradication measures were initiated. Thousands were poisoned, but some had escaped to a nearby island and the process had to be repeated there, also. Control measures continue today.

European hares are large animals that weigh from 6½ to more than 20 pounds, with thick, kinky fur that varies seasonally from brown to gray above. The tail is black on top and white below. Their preferred habitat is open fields and woodlots, and they are fast and agile, making 12-foot bounds when running. Predators find them difficult to pursue and catch.

There is a German myth that claims the goddess of spring, *Eostre*, created the first hare from a bird. To show its gratitude, it began producing eggs during the annual Easter festivals. It was the birth of the Easter Bunny legend.

Snowshoe Hares are also found in the East, but their broad range extends from eastern Canada all the way to Alaska, dipping into New England south to the Alleghenies, the Great Lakes region, from the Northwest south to California and in several of the Rocky Mountain states south to New Mexico.

This is also known as the *varying hare* because of its seasonal changes in color. In the summer it is dark brown above and grayish to white below, while in the winter it is white mottled with brown. The exceptions are in Washington and Oregon, where the hares retain their summer colors year-round.

Snowshoe hares inhabit woodlands, and can run at speeds up to thirty mph. Their young are born with their eyes open and learn to run within a short time. Virtually every predator in the northern regions depends heavily upon the snowshoe hares for food. The population fluctuates from year to year, and once every decade the numbers become exceptionally plentiful. A sharp decline follows, causing lean years and dips in the predator populations, which are closely linked to the availability of this food source.

The tiny **Pygmy Rabbit**, which seldom weighs over 16 ounces, is the smallest of all North American rabbits. It is gray or black above, with a dark tail and white spots on each cheek.

Pygmy rabbits inhabit sagebrush country and create burrow systems in which to live. Sage is the preferred food, and the strong flavor this imparts to the meat makes them undesirable as table fare. Their range includes southeastern Washington, southern Idaho, the southwestern tip of Montana, western Utah, Nevada and a little slice of central California.

Another small species of the West is the **Brush Rabbit**. The fur is a reddish-brown flecked with black, and its ears and legs are short compared to other rabbits. Thick brush is the habitat in which it's most often found. The range is a narrow strip of the western parts of Oregon, California and the Baja.

Nuttall's Cottontail is also called the *mountain cottontail* because of its preference for the uplands. Medium in size, it is grayish-brown above, white below, and has black-tipped ears.

Its range includes central British Columbia; southern Alberta and Saskatchewan; eastern Washington, Oregon and California; and all of the Rocky Mountain states south to New Mexico.

The **Desert Cottontail** is found mostly south

Snowshoe Hare

Desert Cottontail

of the Nuttall's cottontail's range, but there is some overlap. It's a bit larger than its cousin, and has a bright rust-colored nape to go with the buff-brown-above, white-below body.

When available, grasslands are its favorite habitat, but in most places it inhabits desert vegetation.

These rabbits are distributed from California to Texas, and north through the high plains to Montana and South Dakota.

Northern Hares inhabit the open tundra of the western and northern parts of Alaska. Adapting to their environment, they undergo a seasonal change of fur color. In the summer they're gray or brown above, white below and around the eyes, and have black ear tips. The winter coat is all white, but the ear tips remain black. Weights range between 7 and 10 pounds.

Despite the barren country it inhabits, the northern hare manages to forage successfully even throughout the winter when conditions are most severe.

No other native North American hare matches the **Arctic Hare** in body weight, which can reach as high as 15 pounds. It is almost identical to the northern hare in both summer and winter color phases, except that in some places it remains white all year.

Because of their range, which is northern Canada from McKenzie to Newfoundland, few people other than the Indians who inhabit this region get the opportunity to seek them. Their fur and meat are both valuable to the natives, and the main other predator is the arctic fox.

The long ears of the **Black-tailed Jack Rabbit** are what first earned it the name "jackass rabbit," which was eventually shortened to its present form. This is actually a hare instead of a rabbit, since the young are born fully furred and with their eyes open. Adult jack rabbits are

Black-tailed Jack Rabbit

sandy or buff-gray above, liberally sprinkled with black spots, and white below. The tail has a black stripe bordered with white. Weight is between 4 and 8 pounds.

The long, powerful legs help propel this animal at 30 to 35 mph in short bursts, with leaps of 20 feet. When pursued, it occasionally leaps high to survey the surrounding terrain for the best escape routes. It has the tendency to sit very still when danger threatens, apparently trying to decide what course of action to take.

The black-tailed jack rabbit is extremely unpopular with ranchers because it competes with livestock on ranges that have a minimal food supply. For this reason, they're regarded as varmints in many locations and are unprotected by game laws. They also can cause great damage to orchards and farm crops. In periods of high population levels they have been herded into wire enclosures and slaughtered by the thousands.

The native range of this hare is the West, from California and Oregon, east to western Arkansas and Missouri and south to Texas and into Mexico. It has also been introduced into other places such as Nantucket Island and Martha's Vineyard, New Jersey and Kentucky.

White-tailed Jack Rabbits, also true hares, are most prevalent in the midwestern and plains states, but they are distributed from eastern Washington and northeastern California, east to Wisconsin, south to Colorado and north into Alberta and Saskatchewan. The lower part of their range overlaps with that of the black-tailed jack rabbit.

As its name suggests, this animal has a tail that is white both above and below. The body is brown and buff-gray above and white to gray below. Unlike its counterparts, its colors change with the seasons. In the northern part of its range, the long guard hairs drop out and are replaced by white ones. Further south, the summer browns become grayish. Its black-tipped ears and white tail remain the same throughout the year.

The white-tailed species also has long ears and

White-tailed Jack Rabbit

White-tailed Jack Rabbit, winter phase

legs that can move it along at speeds of 36 mph, with spurts of up to 45 mph. It's larger, too, with weights between 5¼ and 9½ pounds. When pursued, it enters water without hesitation and is a strong swimmer. While not welcomed by farmers and ranchers, its territory is smaller and has more plentiful vegetation, so it poses much less of a threat to crops and grasslands.

Antelope Jack Rabbits can make enormous leaps when fleeing predators, a feat which is responsible for their name. The body is gray-brown above, the lower sides white, and the tail black on the upper side. The weights range from 6½ to 9½ pounds. Its long ears work as air conditioning and heating systems. In the summer they are held erect to allow body heat to escape more rapidly. In winter they are kept close to the body to retain warmth.

The range is south-central Arizona and southwest New Mexico, and they are extensively distributed in the arid areas of Mexico.

Closely related and very similar to the antelope jack rabbit, the **White-sided Jack Rabbit** is found only in the extreme southern part of Hidalgo County, New Mexico. The main difference between them is that the antelope jack rabbit has longer ears.

HUNTING METHODS

Of all of the kinds of rabbits and hares in North America, the cottontail is the one most popular with hunters, and considering the huge range the different varieties inhabit, it's no surprise. For example, in the midwestern and plains states alone there are more harvested annually than all other species combined.

Because of the great diversity of geographic locations, habitat and types of terrain rabbits and hares inhabit, there are a number of different hunting techniques. The traditional method is simply walking them up.

There's nothing sophisticated about this approach, and it's the one used by a great many hunters to bag their first bunny. Also, it's democratic in the sense than no special skills or equipment are required. A farm boy stalking the cover with a slingshot has the same chance for success as the hunter toting an expensive double gun or fancy automatic. And although the different species inhabit a wide variety of geographic locations, habitat and terrain, they have the same

basic instincts: to remain perfectly still and hope they are not spotted, or to bolt and run.

Walking up rabbits can be a solo endeavor or one shared by several people, but in either situation, one thing is extremely important:

Move s-l-o-w-l-y!

Rabbits are by nature very nervous creatures, and this trait can be used to great advantage by hunters.

The secret lies in patience. Rabbits will sit tight in cover while hunters walk close by as long as they keep moving. They think they're safe, so they don't budge.

The way to play on their nerves is to build tension. Take three slow steps, then stop and remain still for twenty to thirty seconds. This causes them to suspect they've been detected, and once they get fidgety, they're going to flush and make a dash for freedom.

This also works well for the hunter, because you're anticipating the rabbit's move instead of being surprised when it bursts out.

This slow stop-and-go strategy works well in all kinds of cover that can be easily walked through. It's especially effective in mechanically harvested cornfields where the flattened stalks provide excellent havens for rabbits and a perfect background for their natural camouflage.

This method is the one employed by those rare hunters who are able to consistently spot sitting rabbits. This is an enviable talent, and those who possess it have a great advantage in being able to zero in on the cottontail before it makes a move. The trick is to look for the eye, not the body, since this is the one outstanding feature that isn't camouflaged. Armed with this particular skill, one can bag the rabbit with a slingshot or .22 rifle; and strange as it may seem, there are a very few hunters who can do it with thrown rocks.

It is important for rabbit hunters to maintain a straight line of movement. It's also highly desirable for everyone to wear a blaze orange or brightly colored cap or vest (or both) so they

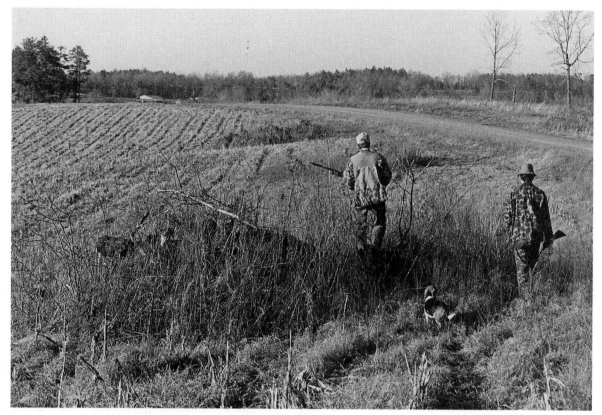

Sinkholes, brushpiles or briar patches are rabbit havens that deserve investigaton. All are tough to penetrate, but worth the effort.

can be easily seen in heavy cover.

As with most wildlife species, there are some variations in rabbit behavior that are related closely to the places they live. Whether it be in the midlands, swamps, desert, snowfields or mountains, there are particular kinds of ploys and strategies they have developed to outwit or confuse their enemies. Local hunters are aware of these, but it might take a visiting nimrod a while to recognize them.

All kinds of cover can harbor rabbits, and not necessarily in large quantity. Rabbits fare very well in suburban areas where minimal cover exists, and usually small plots of cover anywhere in the field are worth investigating. Sinkholes are especially productive, since they are usually located in or nearby agricultural fields. They can't be cultivated, so farmers usually allow them

to grow up in vines, shrubs and saplings. They're hard for stalking hunters to penetrate, but they can be cottontail bonanzas. Sometimes these places are also favored by groundhogs, whose abandoned dens can become rabbit havens, which can tend to curtail hunting success.

Fencerows, once standard on small farms, aren't as numerous now, but they're always worth working thoroughly, especially if they contain some substantial cover. They can pose a disadvantage to a single hunter, because more often than not the animals will go out the opposite side and deny the hunter a chance for a shot. With two or more hunters, both sides can be covered.

Brushpiles are natural targets for hunters, and stomping around atop them will usually drive rabbits out. This won't work on some of the larger ones where it's hard to create enough commotion to inspire an exodus, but it's always worthwhile trying.

Briar patches and honeysuckle thickets can be very difficult if not impossible cover to work. Even if hunters can somehow wade through them, the rabbits inside often simply move around and don't emerge. Hunting these spots is a good way to get well-scratched, frustrated and exhausted. They're better left for dogs, which will be discussed later.

There are times when rabbits can be found in what most observers would consider virtually no cover at all: open green fields of winter wheat or rye grass. The animals seek these places on clear, cold winter days and create very shallow depressions in which they can hunker down with ears flattened back and be nearly impossible to spot until you are only a few yards away. They do this in order to absorb the meager warmth of the winter sun.

Looking over the plot won't reveal anything, even in this very sparse cover. It requires walking over the entire field to jump the animals, because they will hold just as tightly as in heav-

ier cover. There may be a dozen or more cottontails sunning in a field no more than a couple acres in size.

Abandoned or unkept graveyards are great spots to check out, because they're almost always productive. Rabbits like these quiet havens, and perhaps it's because there's usually plenty of luxuriant vegetation. The same thing goes for the perimeters of any deserted structures, whether it be dwellings, barns or other outbuildings around which weeds have grown up. Rabbits also favor as refuges old farm machinery such as hay rakes or discs that have been left to rust, since they, too, are weed-infested and provide barriers against most predators.

Another of the prime cottontail haunts is railroad rights of way, many of which accompany lines that are no longer in service. There's usually good cover at these places. Ideally, one or two hunters can cover each side. A sensible procedure is to leave a second vehicle at or near the place you plan to end the hunt, saving a long trek back to the spot where you started.

The cover along ditches or creek beds is

Rabbit droppings are the best indication that there are animals in the vicinity.

Open fields are always good places to look for rabbits, especially on cold, clear days.

The rights-of-way along railroad tracks are prime rabbit habitat, since they often lie adjacent to fields with agricultural crops.

always worth working, since these are favorite cottontail hides. They like to be near water, and usually there's vegetation available in these moist locations year-round. They're often within close proximity to the fields in which they feed at night, and they are also convenient travel lanes during the daylight hours.

River banks sometimes provide top habitat, particularly in the form of canebrakes that are some of the safest cover rabbits can find. They're safe from winged predators, and the cane stalks are so thickly clustered that larger animals have trouble moving through them. The smaller and lither cottontails can negotiate these mazes with great skill and speed. In addition, by being adjacent to the water, they can swim to safety.

As explained earlier, changing agricultural practices have caused a shift in rabbit populations to new habitat areas. Because of this, hunters should no longer depend on finding them in what were once obvious places. Many locations that used to pay off are now nearly barren of cottontails, and unless you understand what has happened, the outlook may appear bleak. To change this perspective, begin seeking out cover well away from old standbys and sample some of the cover spots you once would have bypassed.

The cottontails have changed, so you must do the same.

A light snowfall can be a hunter's delight, since it allows rabbits to be tracked to their hideaways following a night of feeding and frolic. Of course, tracking is commonplace to those who hunt the snowshoe and arctic hares,

A pair of hunters with two big snowshoe hares taken on a snow-covered farm in North Dakota.

but it's a method unknown to hunters in most of the southern states.

Perhaps the most satisfying and exhilarating way to hunt rabbits is with a good pack of beagles, because having these energetic, short-legged bunny chasers along can add a wonderful dimension to any hunt. The mere sight and sound of these tenacious hounds on the trail of a rabbit is a special thrill, and even if a shot isn't fired, you return home with the feeling of having had a satisfying day afield.

Beagles can bore into cover that defeats hunters. They cover a lot more ground, and since cottontails have the tendency to run in a wide circle, hunters can stand near the place where the rabbit was flushed and be fairly sure it will come back past them sooner or later.

This isn't true of the swamp rabbit, which is more likely to select a straightaway path and follow it until the beagles are out of earshot. Swampers have longer legs than cottontails, and they're considerably faster, so they often evade both dogs and hunters. Their other method of evasion is to enter the water and swim away, and they can easily outdistance a dog. Their smaller cousin, the marsh rabbit, has similar characteristics, so it shows up in hunters' bags a lot less frequently than cottontails.

There are numerous breeds of beagles, some of which date back to early America and beyond,

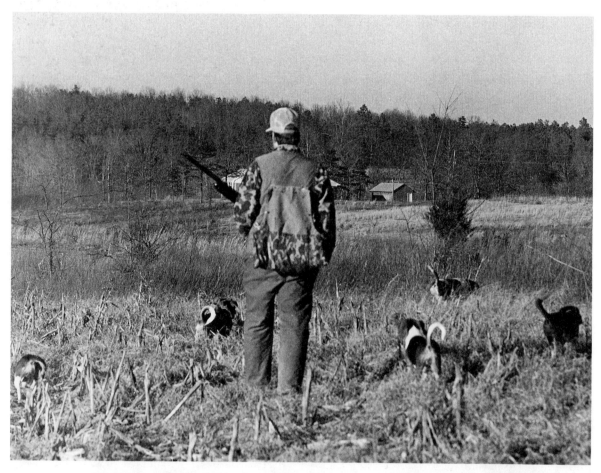

Hunting with beagles increases the enjoyment of the hunt, and boosts the chances for success.

A beagle in pursuit of a cottontail. These short-legged dogs are born to pursue bunnies.

This beagle has chased a rabbit into a burrow and doesn't want to give up.

and it is undoubtedly a point of pride to own a pack of purebreds. However, most hunters are more oriented toward performance, and many mixed breeds do exceedingly well in the field.

In the West, jack rabbits are more or less what individual hunters consider them to be, regardless of how they're classified by the states. To farmers and ranchers, the jacks are considered varmints because of the damage they do to crops and grasslands. On the other hand, sport hunters find them challenging targets, and the younger animals are quite palatable on the table.

Due to the nature of the terrain, much of the hunting is done with rifles, which may range from .22 long rifle to .220 Swift, according to the shooter's ambitions. There are also many

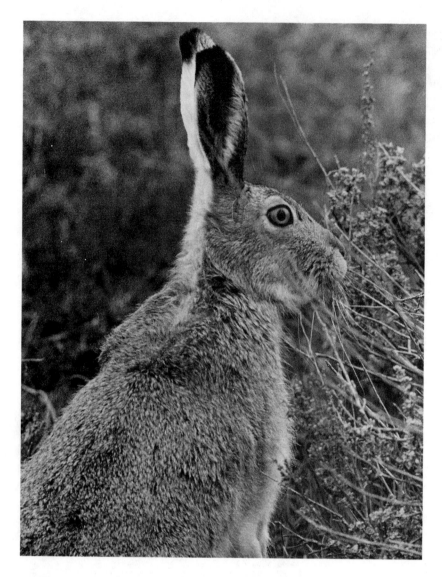

Jack rabbits are very unpopular with western ranchers, as they compete with cattle and sheep for available grass.

handgunners who like to hunt jack rabbits with the high-tech scoped models chambered for high-intensity cartridges. Finally, stalking them in the open country with shotguns can be a real test of skill and reflexes. A flushed jack rabbit can put a lot of distance between itself and a hunter very rapidly!

EQUIPMENT AND ACCESSORIES

Most rabbits are taken with shotguns. The 12 gauge is probably the most-used of all, since it has the greatest range and tosses the largest shot pattern. Both of these factors can be of great

importance at times. The 20 gauge also has a large following, and this is mainly because of two things: first, it's a lot lighter than the 12 gauge (and during a day in the field, this can make a big difference); second, a gun chambered for 3-inch shells, compares favorably with the 12 gauge. The 16 gauge is a great compromise, but sadly, this "in-between" gauge is gradually disappearing from the scene.

Of the smaller gauges, the .410 (which is actually a caliber) and the 28 gauge are both fine choices for beginners, since they have light recoil and give a young shooter confidence in gun handling. There are also skillful hunters

The 12-gauge shotgun is the most popular rabbit gun. Three 12s that are good choices for rabbit hunters are, top to bottom: Winchester Model 1300 pump, Winchester Model 1400 automatic, and Ruger Red Label. All have multi-chokes.

who prefer to use these smaller gauge shotguns in order to add more challenge to the sport.

The use of high brass or low brass shells depends on several things, including the size of the animal and the ranges at which they will be shot. No. 6 is a good all-round choice, since it's large enough to be effective on all rabbits and hares. Smaller shot are okay, but you put a lot

more pellets into the meat than is necessary, and this can be a minor problem at the table.

As for rifles, a pump or automatic .22 long rifle model is enough for cottontails, and the addition of a low-power scope increases accuracy. Similarly, a scope-sighted .22 caliber handgun can be effective in the hands of a trained shooter. The more powerful centerfire .22s aren't recommended for this species.

Footwear is an important item, and it should be chosen with reference to the kind of terrain in which you'll be hunting. Sturdy leather boots with cleated soles are fine for dry or rocky country, while rubber-bottomed pacs are versatile and practical under almost all conditions. Hunters slogging around in marshy places after swamp or marsh rabbits will find knee-high rubber boots very advantageous. Wearing a light pair of cotton socks under the heavier boot socks will help keep the feet drier and more comfortable. It's a good idea to carry along an extra pair of socks in case the others get wet or too damp from walking.

The obstacles rabbit hunters usually encounter require tough outer garments. The coat should be roomy and water repellant, with an ample game bag in the rear, and pants that are double-faced on the legs and seat. Many hunters in the southern states where temperatures are moderate wear only a vest with shell loops and game bag instead of a coat. The hat should be red or blaze orange for personal safety, and a pair of gloves that allow the trigger finger to be free help to keep hands from being scratched while passing through briar patches or thickets.

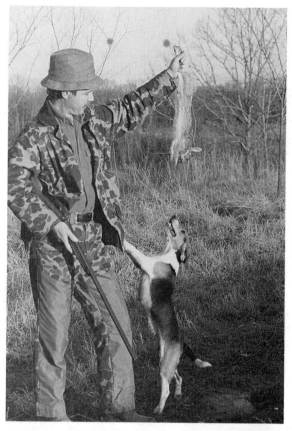

Small-gauge shotguns are okay for rabbits as long as their range capabilities are taken into consideration. This hunter bagged his cottontail with a 28-gauge gun.

The Thompson/Center Kit Gun features both .410 shotgun and .22 Long Rifle barrels, and is made in both adult and youth models. It offers a rabbit hunter the opportunity to switch in the field.

3

Other Animals

Although squirrels, rabbits and hares are by far the most popular of the small-game animals, there are a number of other species that offer hunters additional opportunity. The degree of interest shown in them may vary according to their range and distribution, but several have enthusiastic followings in places where they're most numerous. Too, each represents a separate challenge in terms of methods and tactics used to bag them.

Putting them in the small-game section is an arbitrary decision, since the way they are classified by the various agencies isn't always the same. In different locations they may be designated as game, furbearers, unprotected species or varmints. For example, opossums and skunks are unprotected in Wisconsin and Michigan, while they're listed as game animals in Tennessee and Kentucky. Not infrequently, a species will occupy more than one of these categories, and if so, it may be sought by hunters for different purposes, whether it be for meat, fur or fun. Two of the species, raccoon and skunk, are common carriers of rabies, and when afflicted they often show no fear of man. This is often

mistaken for "friendly" behavior, and children are especially vulnerable, having acquired false impressions of wild animals from television and storybooks. What should be made clear is that it's best to avoid handling any wild animal. It has also been proven that armadillos carry the organism responsible for leprosy, but this doesn't appear to be a threat to humans.

RACCOON

The raccoon, with its bandit's mask and ringed tail, is one of the best-known of the small-game animals, principally because of the apparently "cute" behavior it displays. Depictions of them in cartoons have helped enhance this image. One common misconception is that raccoons wash their food to be sure it's clean, but this isn't correct. They do it to examine what they're holding to be sure it contains no undesirable or foreign objects. There's nothing hygienic about it.

Contrary to the general public's perception, game managers and hunters alike know the raccoon to be one of the most cunning and destructive of the small-game species. If its

Raccoon

Raccoons wash their food, but not for the sake of cleanliness. They're checking for foreign objects.

habits were more widely known, the "cute" reputation would no doubt suffer.

Classed as a carnivore, or meat-eater, the raccoon is actually omnivorous. The range of its diet is very broad, including songbird and waterfowl eggs and fledglings; squirrels, muskrats, young beavers and other small mammals; chickens and other domestic fowl; crawfish, salamanders, snakes, turtles and their eggs; insects, grubs, berries, nuts and numerous farm vegetable crops, particularly corn. They also boldly roam populated areas and forage for whatever they can find. The raccoon has extremely nimble fingers that can pry the lids off garbage cans, open latches and refrigerator doors, and turn doorknobs. Dog and cat food left outside is a favorite target for these nocturnal ramblers.

Raccoons occupy various kinds of habitat, but river bottomlands, lakeshores and wooded areas along streams are preferred. These are locations where many of the food items they consume are found. Dens are usually in hollow trees, but sometimes they are in abandoned animal burrows. The fur of raccoons is valuable and the meat is quite palatable.

'Coon hunting is a nocturnal activity, and the most important ingredient for success is a pack of well-trained hounds. They're essential in the chase, and the aesthetic aspects of listening to

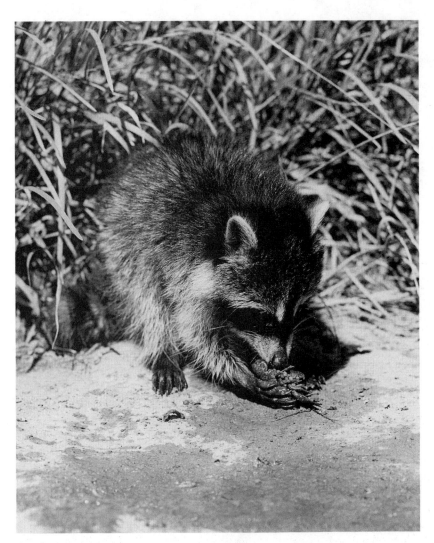

Raccoons are omnivorous, eating almost everything, and crayfish are a staple in their food supply.

A cunning and elusive animal, the raccoon has nimble fingers that can open doors and pry off garbage can lids.

them baying during the chase is where most of the pleasure and satisfaction is gained. Without this element, interest in the sport would diminish sharply and probably die out.

There's a long and colorful history of the various types of hounds that have been used to pursue raccoons. Generally referred to as *tree hounds*, there's no particular breed or mixture that can claim exclusive rights to the territory. However, there are certain blood lines recognized as superior that have been carefully preserved over the years. The buying and selling of 'coon hounds involves big dollars, and a pack of

dogs can be worth a small fortune.

The hunting method is relatively easy to explain. Dogs are released at a selected location, and the hunters usually don't get underway until they hear the sound of them hitting a hot trail. As with rabbits and foxes, this is another sport where the sound of the hounds in pursuit of the quarry is as exciting as the culmination of the hunt.

Once a trail is struck, hunters follow up. In most cases, this means striking out into the darkness and plowing through briars, swamps, thickets, creeks and various other obstacles.

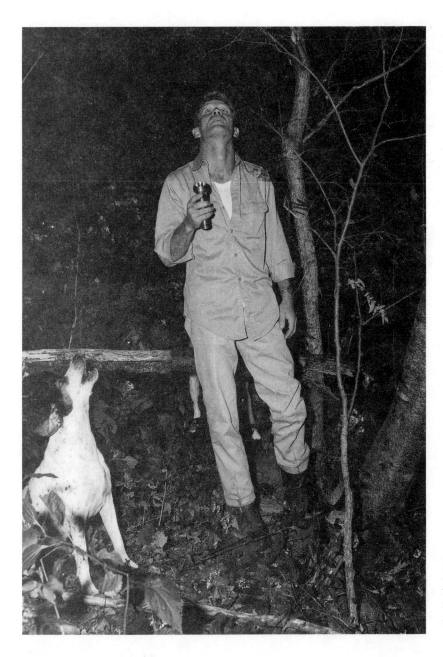

Raccoons are usually hunted at night with dogs, and it can be a rough-and-tumble sport.

When the dogs tree a 'coon, the hunters spot it with a light. Mature animals are harvested and the young ones left alone.

It's a tough sport, but 'coon hunters are a dedicated bunch, and even if they end the night limping, scratched, bleeding, wet and without game, they're smiling. Nonhunters would view this activity as totally mad, but hunters know that 'coon hunting is a sport designed for the hardy.

'Coon-on-a-log contests were once a popular spectator sport for hunters until the practice came under pressure from outside groups that saw it as inhumane. A raccoon was shackled to a floating log and the dog pack was released to go after it. The ensuing battle was usually ferocious, since the raccoon had solid footing and the dogs were swimming. The outcome was usually predictable due to the overwhelming odds. The results are often different in a hunting situation when the two animals meet in the

A 'coon hunter uses a headlight to see while moving through the woods, and to spot the animals when treed.

The right footwear is important when 'coon hunting. Favorites are knee-high rubber boots, waterproof leather boots or rubber-bottomed pacs.

water one-on-one. Raccoons are at home in the water, and their usual tactic is to wrap their legs around a dog's head and drown it.

The best rifles for raccoons are the .22 WRF Magnum, .22 Hornet and .222 Remington, although if the pelts are not a consideration a shotgun with high brass No. 4 loads will do the job very satisfactorily. Knee-high rubber boots

A compact first-aid kit can come in handy on a 'coon hunt when there are lots of briars and barbed-wire fences.

All of these emergency items are worthwhile having along on night hunts, since sometimes a hunter ends up in trouble or in unfamiliar territory.

A light day pack is easy to carry and ideal for including all of the items needed for a night hunt.

and tough, briar-proof clothing are basic necessities. Other important items include a powerful spotlight or head light and a smaller flashlight for traveling through the woods and checking equipment. Lights that attach to a gun barrel are also very useful, since this leaves both hands free when shooting and directs the light precisely on the target. It's also wise to carry a compact first-aid kit to treat injuries suffered by both hunters and dogs. Another handy accessory is a fire-starter kit; on chilly nights it's nice to be able to warm up and dry out between chases or after the hunt.

Raccoons are unprotected in some places, and the hunting seasons vary greatly where they are classed as game. Special dog-training seasons are also sometimes in effect during which no animals can be harvested.

Predator calls can also be used to hunt raccoons, but this will be covered in the varmint section.

The raccoon is widely distributed from the southern edge of the Canadian provinces all through the United States except for some of the Rocky Mountain states and parts of Utah and Nevada. There are two other members of this family. One is the Ringtail or civet cat, which is found throughout the Southwest and in California, southern Oregon, parts of Nevada and Utah and south through Mexico to Central America. Unlike the raccoon, its fur and meat aren't valuable, but man is a principal predator. The other, the Coati, inhabits the southeastern parts of Arizona and New Mexico, southwestern Texas, all of Mexico and into the woodlands of Central America. It also has no commercial value.

OPOSSUM

The Virginia opossum is the subject of many folk tales and jokes, notorious for its "grin" and its habit of feigning death when threatened.

A Virginia opossum and young

This is the only marsupial, or pouched animal, in North America. The opossum is grizzled-gray above, and white below, with whitish face, slender snout and a long, scaly tail. Its size is similar to that of a large house cat.

Open woods and overgrown areas are favored habitat, but it isn't unusual for them to invade urban areas to raid garbage cans. In the wild, they're not discriminating and eat carrion, snakes, frogs, salamanders, small mammals, berries, fruit and various crops, particularly corn. They inhabit hollow logs, abandoned burrows, caves or practically any site that offers shelter. 'Possums feed mostly at night, and great numbers of these slow-moving, clumsy creatures are run over by vehicles on the highways. Their taste for road kills may have something to do with this. They *become* what they're looking for.

Opossums are sought for both fur and meat, the latter being considered a delicacy by some people. Because of their affinity for carrion, many prefer to capture them alive, then hold them in pens and feed them a diet of vegetable matter to clean out their digestive tract and improve the meat. In recent years the fur has been of little value, so the species is paid less attention by trappers. Hunters use dogs to find and tree the animals, but sometimes in the fall, when persimmons are ripe, they go afield seeking them with only lanterns or flashlights. Persimmons are a favorite food of other animals, particularly raccoons, which no doubt gave rise to the old Southern ditty:

'Possum in a 'simmon tree,
Raccoon on the ground.
Raccoon say "You son-of-a-gun!
Shake them 'simmons down!"

The opossum's range has expanded since the first settlers arrived, and includes most of the eastern United States except Maine, northern Michigan and northern Minnesota; southwest to Colorado and parts of Arizona and Texas; and in the coastal areas of the West from British Columbia to California.

A .22 rimfire rifle is sufficient for opossums, and if they are shaken out of a tree or cornered on the ground, a stick will put them in their state of faked death and they can be picked up and tossed into a burlap sack.

ARMADILLO

The nine-banded armadillo enjoys the colloquial nickname of "'possum on the half-shell," but this is a misnomer. While the two species are somewhat alike in appearance, and both are candidates for the title "King of the Road Kills," they're not at all related. Each occupies a separate order, and in the United States each is the single member within that category. The shell is tan to black, with sparse hair sprouting between the plates. It has a small head and a long, tapering tail.

Spanish conquistadores first encountered this strange-looking creature in Mexico and called it "little man in armor." It's an apt name, since it's the only living mammal with bony shell plates.

Armadillos may be on the move at anytime during the night or day, scurrying around and rooting in vegetation for food or digging the burrows in which they live. Their main diet consists of insects, grubs, worms, salamanders, crawfish, eggs of birds and reptiles, and carrion. They appear slow and clumsy, but are surprisingly fast and agile.

While not seriously pursued by hunters, these animals are quite good to eat. The meat has the flavor of pork or chicken. Tourists to some of the areas where they are found are offered baskets, bowls and handbags made from the shells. Although they roam during the day, most hunting for them takes place at night when they're most active. They often supplement the bag of 'possum and 'coon hunters. Unlike the opossum, which plays dead when cornered, the armadillo rolls up into a tight, nearly impenetrable ball.

Armadillos migrated into the United States from Mexico and have spread widely through

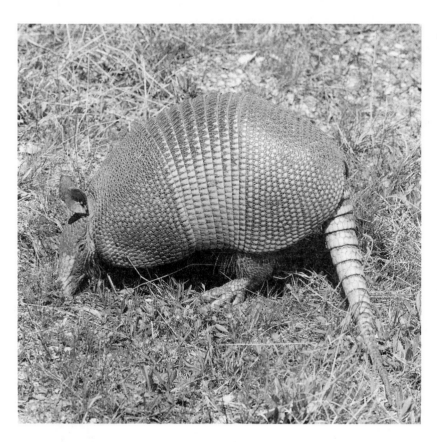

Armadillo

the southeastern states. They were deliberately introduced into Florida in the 1920s, and now their range extends from that state through the southern parts of Georgia, Alabama, Mississippi, Louisiana, Arkansas, Kansas and much of Texas. Since they don't hibernate and can't survive extended periods of freezing weather, geography will eventually establish a range limit.

SKUNK

The skunk is in a family that also includes weasels, otters, badgers, minks and fishers, and there are four species represented. The most widely distributed of these is the striped skunk, which is found in almost all of the United States and in many of the Canadian provinces. The eastern spotted skunk's range includes Minnesota and South Dakota and south to Texas and Louisiana; and, in the East, Illinois and central Pennsylvania south to Mississippi, west-

ern South Carolina and Florida. The two other species, hooded skunk and hog-nosed skunk, have limited range in the southwestern states.

Skunks are omnivorous and eat small mammals, bird eggs, amphibians, grubs, insects, berries and a wide variety of vegetable matter. In urban areas, skunks cause lawn damage when rooting for insects, and occasionally they will take up residence under houses. They're also notorious for invading campsites.

Mostly nocturnal, skunks spend the daylight hours in hollow logs, burrows abandoned by other animals, crevices or brushpiles. They do not hibernate, but they may remain dormant during periods of severe weather.

Although a gentle, harmless creature by nature, the skunk is a formidable adversary when threatened. It is equipped with anal glands that contain a potent musk that can be sprayed at intruders, which is usually sufficient to deter further action. The smell is distinctive, and few people are unacquainted with it, either as a result of personal contact or through literature or movies. In early western films, the skunk's nickname *polecat* was commonly applied to unsavory characters.

The pelts of skunks are valuable, so it has been a prime target for trappers over the years. Small-game hunters have sought them for the same reason, usually with the assistance of a dog. Earlier in the century, there were skunk hounds bred and trained specifically for locating and baying the animals. The hunter would follow up and check the pelt to see if it was worth taking. Since fur with too much white had little value, such animals were usually left unharmed.

Hunters are sometimes sprayed in unexpected encounters with skunks, an experience that is never forgotten. The intensity of the odor at close range is sufficient to cause vomiting. The best scent neutralizers are tomato juice or ammonia, followed by washing the skin with a strong carbolic soap.

MUSKRAT

Both the common muskrat and the round-tailed muskrat are generally thought of as animals sought primarily for their fur, but there are those who like the meat and hunt them for this purpose alone. In weight they range from 1¼ to 4 pounds.

While the round-tailed muskrat is found only in southeastern Georgia and throughout the Florida Peninsula, the common muskrat's range is extensive in North America. They're found everywhere except the arctic regions of Canada; parts of California and a few southwestern states, including Texas; and Georgia and Florida. They inhabit creeks, rivers, canals, marshes, ponds and lakes.

Muskrats feed primarily on aquatic vegetation, but will on occasion eat fish, clams, mussels and crayfish. In the wild, their main enemies are raccoons and mink, which open up muskrat houses and devour the young.

Muskrat

The meat of muskrats, often called *marsh rabbit*, is good eating, and at one time it was fairly popular and was sold commercially. One of the best ways to harvest muskrats is to locate yourself near a stream, river or lake that you know they inhabit and pick them off with a scope-sighted .22 rimfire or .22 WRF Magnum rifle. They move about during daylight hours, and all that's required to bag them is patience and the ability to hit a swimming target.

NUTRIA

This larger version of the muskrat was introduced in Louisiana from South America in the 1930s in an effort to boost the fur market. Eventually it spread into surrounding states. It was also introduced in Washington and Ore-gon, some Great Plains states, Maryland and New Jersey.

Nutria are similar to the muskrat in most ways except for size—they can be up to five times as big. Because of this, those who find them good table fare get some hefty portions when they bag one. These animals become pests when populations are high, causing damage to stream banks and overbrowsing vegetation along waterways.

BEAVER

Anyone familiar with American history is well acquainted with the part beavers played in the opening of new routes of travel and centers of commerce as the westward movement continued. Because of their valuable fur, they were

Beaver

A beaver lodge in winter. The animals are curled up inside, cozy and warm, with an abundance of stored food.

the prime goal of trappers who continued to probe into new and unexplored areas in search of them. It was a relentless campaign, and trapping continued unregulated until it resulted in the animal disappearing from much of its original range. Since that time, beavers have become well reestablished all over North America, and in many places their numbers are greater than anytime in the past. The only places devoid of them are California, Nevada and Florida.

Beavers feed primarily on the bark of trees, but they also eat tubers and other vegetation growing close to the water areas they inhabit. They have become classified as varmints or pests in some places because the dams they build flood out valuable commercial timber and croplands. To combat this problem, there are now professional beaver exterminators for hire, a stark contrast from the days when they were so highly prized.

A good example of this exists in Manitoba, Canada, where beavers have greatly increased in numbers and have wreaked havoc throughout the province. They have built dams that have flooded highways and grain fields, and in addition, felled the poplar trees farmers plant as windbreaks. While the principal amount of damage has been in Manitoba, beavers have also invaded the suburban areas in heavily populated southwestern Ontario, damming small creeks and streams, which has led to the flooding of stands of trees.

With fur prices too low to give trappers incentive, the government has spent hundreds of thousands of dollars in beaver control measures, but to little avail. Blowing up dams is only a temporary deterrent, since they can rebuild them in a very short time. Officials say beavers are winning the battle, so it's anybody's guess as to what the future holds.

Other than man, the only natural enemies of the beaver are the bear and wolf, neither common enough throughout their range to make inroads in the population. Beavers can weigh up to 80 pounds, and a big adult is more than a dog or coyote can handle.

The meat of beavers is very good, and the fatty tail is considered a delicacy in the northern parts of the continent.

PORCUPINE

Nearly everyone has seen or heard of the porcupine, an animal unique in North America because the sharp quills it carries as defensive weapons. Slow-moving and nonaggressive, this animal has few enemies except for a few carnivores who have the ability to get at its soft underparts without getting peppered with quills. Their range is Canada, Alaska, and most of the western United States; northern Minnesota, Michigan and Wisconsin; and New England south to New York and Pennsylvania.

The porcupine's diet consists of leaves, tree bark, clover, and various kinds of woodland vegetation. It is also fond of salt and is notorious for chewing wooden and leather goods that have absorbed human perspiration.

There's not much incentive for hunters to go after porcupines unless they happen to be lost or incapacitated and truly desperate for something to eat. The animals are easy prey, since all it takes to kill them is a sharp blow on the nose. All things considered, potting them from a distance with a .22 rifle might be a better choice of action. The Indians used the quills for decoration and also ate the meat.

4

Modern Varmint Hunting

There have always been birds and animals in this country that were considered varmints, so it's also accurate to say that there have always been varmint hunters. Youngsters potting away at English sparrows or starlings with a BB gun, or shooting rats and other small rodents with a .22 rifle qualified, as did the farmer who considered all hawks "chicken hawks" and who also had to contend with weasels, foxes, skunks and other pests. And there are few hunters who haven't taken shots at some varmints during their time in the field.

Early varminters used the large-bore rifles that were traditional for all kinds of shooting at that time, and it wasn't until the late 1800s that efforts were made to get away from the big, heavy, hard-kicking models. Breech-loading rifles with self-contained cartridges were fairly new to the scene, although none were much smaller than .40 caliber. The departure from this standard was initiated by a small group of target shooters in the New England states who began to experiment with small-caliber cartridges for pests.

The main pest that spurred the effort was the woodchuck. This region was heavily populated, and hunting opportunities were limited, but those hungry for more action discovered that the abundant woodchucks offered great potential for additional sport. The problem was that most landowners weren't eager to have hunters on their property banging away with big-bore guns, and it became obvious that the only solution was to create rifles that were less noisy and better suited for the purpose.

EARLY VARMINT CARTRIDGES

By today's standards, the cartridges weren't impressive, but they led to the recognition of varmint hunting as a sport and the new pest rifles as a separate class of firearms. The new cartridges were the .22 WCF (Winchester centerfire), .22/ 15/60 Stevens and .25/20 or .25/21 Stevens, all of which combined small bullets and large cartridges that could accommodate the blackpowder charges needed to propel the bullets at high velocities. The performance of these cartridges was enhanced by matching them up with the single-shot *schuet-*

According to their size and the distances at which they're shot, varmints are hunted with everything from .17 caliber pellet guns to high-intensity cartridges like the .220 Swift.

zen rifles produced by Stevens, Winchester and Ballard that were the favorites of target shooters. Not surprising, these were the same people who became the first dedicated varmint hunters.

The early cartridges had several limitations, one of which was that the small bullets had a very poor trajectory. They were okay up to about 100 yards, but after that the rate of drop was enormous. Little was known about bullet design and how it influenced velocity and trajectory and how this in turn affected accuracy. Also, target shooters' inclination to stick with black powder as a propellant was a disadvantage. Smokeless powder was available, but favored by reloaders. When it was accepted in the early 1900s some interesting cartridges showed up that were to have real impact on subsequent developments.

The most impressive of these newcomers was the .22 Savage High-Power, introduced in 1912. It had greater muzzle velocity than its predecessors, and the performance was much more suitable for shooting at longer ranges. Because of poor marketing strategy, it never had a chance to prove itself to the public.

Another that had great potential was the 6mm Lee Navy, a cartridge originally designed for the 1895 Lee rifle that was used for a time by the U.S. Navy. Because hunters considered this a target-shooting cartridge, it wasn't given much attention. The irony is that only minor changes were necessary to convert the original Navy case into the .220 Swift, still one of the greatest varmint cartridges ever.

The era of what can be called modern varmint hunting began in the late 1920s with the appearance of the .22 Hornet. There is irony here, also, because the developers of this cartridge, Townsend Whelen and G.L. Wotkyns, used the obsolete .22 WCF case along with jacketed bullets and smokeless powder to produce what is still regarded as a phenomenal little cartridge for medium-range varmint work.

One of the principal differences between the .22 Hornet and its predecessors was that it was the first to be promoted strictly as a varmint round, and this faced most manufacturers with a problem. They didn't think varmint hunting was popular enough to warrant all-out promotion, so they chose a sort of sit-back-and-wait attitude. At first, most .22 Hornets were the result of rechambering of the Model 1922 Springfield .22 rimfire rifles, but the most exposure was through the Model 54 Winchester and Savage's Model 23D.

The man responsible for focusing the public's attention on varmint hunting was Townsend Whelen. At the time he was a contributing editor for *Outdoor Life* magazine and very well respected in the shooting community. Helpful also was the growing awareness of hunters of the shrinking seasons and bag limits for most game species, which fueled their desire to find other shooting outlets. Varmint shooting was the only choice for a year-round sport.

The evolution of varmint hunting to the level of sophistication it has reached today has been due in large part to the contributions of benchrest shooters. It has been this group of highly skilled and talented individuals upon whom varmint hunters have always depended for improvements in the design and performance of both cartridges and rifles. And once varmint hunting proved itself to manufacturers, they became very cooperative, producing the rifles and ammunition that showed special promise.

Not long after the .22 Hornet appeared on the scene, two of the country's leading experimenters, Jerry Gebby and G.L. Wotkyns, were looking toward much hotter cartridges that would attain previously unheard-of velocities. Their work led to Winchester introducing the legendary .220 Swift in 1935, with an astounding 4100 fps muzzle velocity. Yet this cartridge became bogged down in a morass of controversy, misunderstanding and misinformation that doomed it to be virtually shelved for many years. For instance, one prominent writer claimed that the Swift cartridge "followed no rules in reloading," and that the slightest irregularities in the load would cause pressures to rise to astronomical heights. The charge of excessive barrel wear was leveled by another writer. Neither assertion was true, and even though nothing in the field compared with the Swift's performance, the adverse publicity prevented its real potential from being realized by shooters.

All the while, benchrest shooters were constantly experimenting with various "wildcat" cartridges. Many of these never became commercially available, yet each usually made a contribution of some sort and helped advance the technology. The same still goes on today, although almost all of the possible options have been exhausted. There is one prominent exception which will be mentioned shortly.

It would be impossible to list all of the persons responsible for the advancements in varmint cartridges during this period. However, in addition to those already mentioned, J.B. Smith, Harvey Donaldson, Hervey Lovell, Leslie Lindahl, Lysle Kilbourn and P.O. Ackley were particularly significant.

The Europeans had also been at work developing new cartridges, but those they produced were far better suited for game larger than varmints, since there are few small animals to hunt in those countries. The best known of the European cartridges were the 5.6×61 Vom Hofe Super Express and the 5.6×35R Vierling. They also used the .22 Savage High-Power round, which was know as the 5.6×52R. The British .240 Apex was a hot 6mm cartridge that would have been all right for varmints, but such creatures were of no interest there. None of these cartridges generated any interest whatsoever in America.

There were other commercial calibers produced during the 1930s that were of some importance but not of lasting popularity. Among these were the .218 Bee, .219 Zipper, .25/20 and .32/20. Marlin currently produces a lever gun in all of these calibers except the .219 Zipper, and ammunition remains available.

THE POSTWAR ERA

A true sea change occurred in the sport of varmint hunting in 1950 when Remington introduced its terrific .222 with a 3200 fps muzzle velocity, because it was the first of a succession of super-accurate varmint rifles that would raise the sport to a much higher level and attract new hunters by the thousands.

The .222 quickly became the most popular varmint cartridge of all time. Because it was entirely new, rather than an update or reconfiguration of a previous cartridge, it represented a refreshing change.

Something else: the event marked the entry of Remington into the varmint field, which until this time had been dominated by Winchester. Also, the .222's instant popularity wasn't lost on European gunmakers, who were eager to take advantage of the varmint hunter's appetite for this new caliber. It was this recognition that resulted in the magnificent Sako, Krico and other fine rifles showing up on the American market.

There's little doubt that the .222 Remington brought large numbers of new varmint and benchrest shooters into the fold. The .222 was

An ideal long-range varmint outfit: Ruger .223 caliber Varminter; 6.5×-20× Leupold scope; Harris Bipod; and Leupold 9×35 Porro binoculars.

highly accurate and comfortable to shoot, devoid of the kind of muzzle blasts produced by some of the other calibers. It was popular both on the target range and in the field. Warren Page, who was the shooting editor for *Field & Stream*, gave the .222 an enormous amount of publicity, since he was deeply involved in benchrest shooting as well as varmint hunting. A later version of this cartridge, the .222 Magnum, had a brief history, mainly because it didn't comfortably fit into the existing pattern of varmint calibers.

The next important step by Remington was the .223 cartridge, 3240 fps, which is by far one of the most successful rounds of all time. It was manufactured for both civilian and military use, with the latter being classified as 5.56 ammunition. The .223 is excellent for long-range varmint hunting and has been very competitive with the .222 in capturing the hearts of benchrest shooters.

In terms of muzzle velocity, the .222 and .223 are almost identical, so performance doesn't give either an edge. However, the easy availability of less expensive military ammunition has definitely had a bearing on shooters deciding between the two at point of purchase.

The next two cartridges to appear were the .243 Winchester and .244 Remington. Both are 6mm caliber, and except for the long-ago Lee Navy cartridge, they were the first 6mm rounds to be seen by most Americans.

Winchester's .243 was the first out of the gate, and with a 3,500 fps velocity, it was second in this category only to the .220 Swift in conventional rifles. Weatherby had a .257 Magnum, but only that company loaded ammunition for it.

It didn't take long for the .243 to gain popularity, and as more manufacturers began producing rifles chambered for this cartridge, the surge of interest mushroomed.

Remington's .244 followed, and while plenty of competition developed between the two rounds, it was the .243 that eventually triumphed. Winchester went after both varmint and deer hunters in their sales campaigns, and both fell in love with the sleek, beautifully crafted and accurate Winchester Model 70. Remington's Model 722 simply couldn't divert their attention sufficiently to make it feasible to continue production. The .244's life span was only five years.

Other calibers bit the dust soon after these 6mm rounds appeared. Manufacturers ceased making rifles chambered for the .257 Roberts, .250 Savage and .220 Swift, and although two of these would later reappear, they were absent for quite a while.

One of the oldies in the crowded field of wildcatting was the .22/250, an extremely fast and efficient cartridge dating back to 1930. Benchrest shooters prized this highly accurate cartridge, but amazingly, the firearms manufacturers ignored it until the mid-1960s when Remington adopted the round and began producing ammunition. While Browning had the first .22/250 rifle on the commercial market, Remington was soon in competition with two chambered for it: a Model 700 and the superb 40-× target rifle. This satisfied both field and benchrest shooters, and they were soon in wide use. The result was that several other manufacturers, domestic and foreign, began building .22/250 rifles.

This finally established the .22/250 in the place it always belonged: in the same league with the best-performing varmint cartridges of our time. It has accumulated a huge following, and rightly so!

The .220 Swift is also back, but still not on a scale that's anywhere near what it deserves to be. The Swift is the top-stepper of the varmint cartridges, with a better than 4,100 fps velocity. On the commercial market, it's available from Remington in their Model 700 and from Ruger in both the classic No. 1 and Model 77, the latter of which is an extremely fine varmint rifle by

The Ruger No. 1 in .220 Swift gives the varmint shooter the ultimate capability that can be obtained with commercial cartridges. The bullet zips along at more than 4,000 fps.

The Weatherby .224 Magnum is a popular varmint rifle that has excellent long-range capabilities.

anybody's standards. A couple of manufacturers supply commercial loads.

Weatherby produced two varmint cartridges, the .224 Magnum and the .240 Magnum. Both are fine performers, and the .240 is capable of taking down animals larger than varmints. Despite the excellence of both of these rounds, neither enjoys the high profile exhibited by most of the other varmint calibers. That's because the rifles are quite expensive. Many shooters dream of owning a Weatherby but settle for something they can better afford.

An interesting varmint cartridge that still may someday enjoy more popularity than it has attained so far is the .17 Remington, which tosses a tiny 25-grain bullet out of the muzzle at better than 4,000 fps. There have been a number of .17 caliber wildcat cartridges around for a long time, some of which gained considerable recognition, but no commercial rifle or ammu-

nition was produced until the .17 Remington appeared in 1971.

This little caliber has lots going for it in terms of speed and accuracy, because it compares favorably with the .22/250 in some respects. It is also an efficient and quiet rifle for woodchucks and crows, and the small bullet is sufficient to do a thorough job on either of these. Its one disadvantage is that, owing to its light weight, it's easily deflected by wind. Somehow, the .17 was never embraced by varmint shooters, so it has been virtually relegated to the

A variety of varmint ammunition. Top, left to right: .32-20 Winchester, .25-20 Winchester, .218 Bee, .22 Hornet, .222 Remington, .17 Remington, .223 Remington, .22-250 Remington, .224 Weatherby, .243 Winchester, .220 Swift, .25-06 Remington. Bottom, left to right: .177 precision match pellet, .177 pointed field pellet, .22 precision match pellet, .22 Long Rifle solid, .22 Long Rifle hyper-velocity, .22 Long Rifle hollowpoint, .22 Long Rifle bird shot, .22 Winchester Magnum hollowpoint, .22 Winchester Magnum full metal jacket.

wings. But it's still being produced, and perhaps it will be better received by a future generation of shooters.

Shooters who own a .30/06 rifle and have a yen to use it on varmints can do so with Remington's Accelerator cartridge, which is nothing more than a .22 bullet encased in a plastic sleeve, called a sabot, the size of the bore. When fired, the bullet and sabot separate shortly after leaving the muzzle and the .22 bullet goes on its way. Though not capable of pinpoint accuracy, the Accelerator is okay for larger varmints like coyotes, or for woodchucks at closer ranges.

As noted, experimentation with wildcat cartridges has been the major force in advancing target and varmint shooting to its present position. This isn't carried on as avidly as it once was because so many avenues have already been explored. However, there are still plenty of target and varmint shooters who prefer the wildcats over the calibers available on the commercial market. Too, as with almost everything else in the field of science (and target and varmint shooting are definitely in that arena), new and exciting things continue to occur—and the future may hold even more.

Today, the most popular of the wildcats is the .22 CHeetah, a cartridge designed by Jim Carmichel, shooting editor for *Outdoor Life*, and Fred Huntington, founder of RCBS, which makes reloading tools. The round moves out at the astonishing velocity near 4,300 fps, and performs ideally for long-range target and varmint shooting. Two major custom gunmakers, the Shilen Rifle Company and Wichita Engineering, are producing finished rifles in .22 CHeetah.

The cartridge evolution has been accompanied by equally impressive developments in the firearms built to accommodate them. The sophisticated, ultra-accurate rifles available today are an enormous advance over the early pest guns and are capable of delivering high-intensity rounds precisely in extended-range varmint or target shooting.

It didn't begin that way, of course. At the outset, the major emphasis was on cartridge development rather than accuracy. Typically, varmints were shot at fairly close range, so pinpoint accuracy wasn't of great importance. Ironically, some of the early experimental cartridges had potential far beyond the rifles' capability.

What brought attention to the importance of accuracy was the "benchrest connection," those varmint hunters who were also target shooters. They knew that a cartridge was no better than the firearm from which it was delivered, so their focus was on this aspect of performance.

Benchrest rifles were heavy and cumbersome, with long barrels and stocks that were little more than big blocks of wood intended to supply solid support. Initially, it was believed that the main keys were the bullet and the barrel. If the bullet was right and the barrel straight and true with smoothly finished lands and grooves, a marksman's eye could do the rest.

At fairly short ranges, this premise held water, but as shooting distances were increased it became obvious that a lot more factors were involved. One of the first discoveries was that bullet performance was greatly influenced by how the rifle was fitted into the stock. It was learned that a "floated barrel," one that did not touch the wood, was more accurate, thus the science of properly bedding the rifle into the stock was born. Likewise, if the action wasn't properly seated, minor twisting could influence bullet flight. Today's excellent synthetic stocks allow gunmakers to accomplish bedding to a degree of perfection not possible with wood, and although the aesthetics aren't the same, the bottom line—performance—can't be argued.

These changes came about gradually. As varmint hunters paid more attention to the matter of accuracy, their bond with the benchrest shooters continued to solidify. While much of the credit goes to the benchrest shooters, it wasn't entirely a one-way street; each was making important contributions, and progress was accelerated by combining forces and sharing information.

Of course, improvements in all aspects of benchrest and varmint rifles are continuing. Once it was recognized that each of the rifle's components represented an area of specialization, advancement was accelerated. In the custom and commercial fields there were craftsmen and engineers concentrating solely on particular parts: barrels, actions, triggers or stock design.

TODAY'S RIFLES

The varmint rifle as we know it today evolved from this collaboration. The kind of firearm practical for field use varies considerably from what is necessary for precision target shooting, yet by combining forces and utilizing the products created by advanced technology, better "recipes" are constantly being created. As a side note, there is a NASA connection: some of the knowledge of ballistics gained by shooters aided NASA's space flight program, and materials developed for this program have in turn been useful to gunmakers and shooters.

Winchester and Savage were the first manufacturers to get into the varmint rifle field once the .22 Hornet appeared, but it was some time before they understood that bolt-action rifles were by far the best for long-range shooting. Both made some lever-action models that didn't do justice to the cartridges for which they were chambered. Before commercial rifles were available, most were custom conversions from military models, and benchrest guns were all custom made.

The picture remained essentially the same for quite a few years, but after World War II there was an upsurge of interest in varmint hunting. This got the attention of other gunmakers, and the competition stiffened. Remington made a major move into the field, and with the success of its .222, became extremely high profile.

In addition to these three, many other manufacturers have been in the varmint rifle business through the years. Of the domestic companies, the names that are best known are Ruger, Browning, Weatherby, Dakota, Colt, Mossberg, Marlin, Kimber, Harrington & Richardson, Stevens, Ithaca and Smith & Wesson. Some of these firms are no longer in business, and a couple others have dropped their rifle lines.

As for the foreign gunmakers, the Belgian firm, Fabrique Nationale, was one of the first to enter the U.S. market. Later, the superb Finnish Sako rifles took varmint shooters by storm, and Sako actions were widely used by other manufacturers. Others followed, of which Krico, Anschutz, BSA, Mannlicher, Kleinguenther, Husqvarna, Mauser, Charles Daly, Heckler & Koch and Interarms are the most familiar.

The quality of many of the commercial firearms is first rate, and some are of superior quality, but a varmint hunter seeking the ultimate in a rifle will end up doing business with a custom gunmaker. There are several outstanding companies in the United States, and their products are without peer anywhere in the world.

A custom rifle represents the finest in technology, engineering and handcrafting; but more than that, it is created specifically for the client in terms of weight, balance, stock material and design, trigger pull, recoil management and ornamentation. The difference in the feeling of mounting a custom rifle and one off the rack in a sporting goods store is similar to that of trying on a tailor-made suit after always having worn ones bought in a department store.

There are many custom gunmakers, most of which use the very best component parts available to assemble their rifles; but a few build the entire product themselves. Also, custom makers can chamber a rifle for whatever the client desires. There are still many shooters who prefer particular wildcat cartridges, and custom rifles are the only solution other than conversions.

While it's logical that small-bore rifles will always dominate the varmint shooting field, it's

A selection of varmint outfits. Left to right: Savage 112FV in .22-250 and Simmons 6×-20× scope; Winchester Model 70 Sporter in .22-250 and Bausch & Lomb 6×-24× scope; Winchester Model 70 Varmint in .223 and Leupold 3.5×-10× scope; Ruger Varminter in .223 and Leupold 6.5×-20× scope; Remington Model 700 Varmint in .22-250 and Redfield 4×-12× scope; Ruger Model 77 Mark II in .243 and Leupold 2×-7× scope; and Weatherby Mark V in .224. and Weatherby 2×-7× scope.

worthwhile mentioning that there's also limited potential for big bores in the overall picture. Varmints are occasionally hunted with cartridges designed for game as large as elephants, such as the .458 Win. Magnum, .404 Jeffreys, .416 Rigby and .375 H&H Magnum, and other big boomers like the .340 Weatherby Magnum, .300

H&H Magnum, .338 Winchester and .45/70 Government aren't strangers to the sport.

It may not make sense at first glance, but there are valid reasons why these heavy-duty cartridges are used. One is that big-game hunters usually have little opportunity to use their large-bore rifles. Shooting varmints provides a way to keep

A contrast in varmint cartridges: a .416 Rigby (left) and a .224 Weatherby Magnum.

in practice and feel comfortable handling this type of firearm. Whatever kind of varmint they go after is much smaller than the game they will be seriously hunting, so if they can consistently score on them, they can feel confident of their marksmanship. Another is that some hunters just enjoy firing the heavy kickers occasionally, and varmints are a greater challenge and more fun than plinking away on a target range.

Incidentally, this big-bore varmint shooting isn't restricted to rifles. Many handgunners are involved for the same reasons.

Finally, it doesn't take much thought to come to the conclusion that you can't *overgun* any varmint, and that there's little difference in the results of hitting a prairie dog or a woodchuck with a .220 or a .458. Both are devastating.

A majority of serious long-range varmint

Reloading is very popular among varmint hunters, since it allows them to experiment with different loads and bullets.

shooters do their own reloading. There are several reasons for this, and while economy is surely one, the ability to experiment with different bullets and powder charges is also of great importance. Reloaders can also work up new loads of their own design, and this helps to determine the ones that perform the best at various ranges and for miscellaneous kinds of varmints.

Reloading can add much to the enjoyment of either varmint or target shooting, but it is something that requires great discipline and attention to detail. Matters of weight and measurements are of extreme importance, and often a gram of powder can put a load over or under the prescribed limits.

There are numerous companies that manufacture and market reloading equipment, as well as all of the necessary component materials. Also, there are several dependable manuals that fully describe standard and alternate loads for all commercial and many wildcat cartridges, and reloaders should refer to all of them when checking out information on any load in order to see if there are alternate formulas.

Expense isn't an obstacle, because basic reloading tools can be purchased at a quite moderate price, and these sets are best for the beginner. Learning from the bottom up is beneficial and helps a handloader to better understand the principles and limitations involved.

TELESCOPE SIGHTS

Cartridges and rifles have been discussed, but there's a third element without which long-range varmint and target shooting wouldn't be possible: the telescopic sight.

No matter how well a cartridge performs, or how accurately a rifle can deliver the bullet, long-range shooting is impossible without optical assistance in the form of what is commonly referred to as a rifle scope. Put simply, this is a device that compresses the distance between the shooter and the target through magnification,

providing the opportunity for precise bullet placement. Like Sam Colt's famous revolver, it's an "equalizer" that allows both young and old eyes to see the target on the same plane and to focus clearly.

Telescopic sights have been around for a long time, although not in the form we are using today. The earliest scopes had long, thin tubes that extended almost the entire length of the barrels, which at that time were pretty long. These rudimentary optics were employed mainly by the military, in this country and abroad. During the Civil War, telescopic sights were used by snipers on both sides. After the conflict, scopes were adopted by target shooters, but even though the optics were very good and their performance quite creditable, the instruments were delicate and not sturdy enough for hunters to use in the field. Varmint and small-game hunters relied on open or peep sights.

Hunting scopes began showing up on the American market around the turn of the century. Most were produced by German and Austrian firms, of which there were several; but two in particular—Zeiss and Kahles—are still quite familiar to target shooters and hunters. These first scopes were similar in appearance to those being produced today, and some were of surprisingly fine quality. But they weren't fogproof and waterproof, didn't have coated lenses, and lacked the sophisticated internal adjustments now considered standard. The magnification range was from 2× to 5×, with the same basic choice of reticles: post, duplex, crosshair and dot.

Even after this kind of scope became available, varmint hunters didn't flock to buy them, choosing instead to continue to use open and peep sights. Two things came about in the early 1930s that turned some heads. First, a German-American technician named Rudolph Noske created a rifle scope with internal adjustments and long eye relief, solving two of the shooter's most nagging problems. Second, Bill Weaver began producing a line of high-quality, mod-

This Remington 40XB with a Lyman 10× Super Targetspot scope is still considered by many shooters to be one of the finest benchrest combinations.

estly priced scopes that the average hunter could afford. It was revolutionary, because until that time, scopes were owned mostly by well-heeled sportsmen. Most important, the cost of Weaver scopes and mounts made all manufacturers, domestic and foreign, compete on the low rather than the high end of the price spectrum.

This didn't eliminate the high-ticket scopes, of course, because benchrest and varmint hunters serious about the ultimate in accuracy at long range still look toward the finest models available. Two early favorites were the 15× Lyman Super Targetspot and the Unertl 12× Ultra Varmint scope, which some still consider to be the best in their class. Yet today's state-of-the-art scopes overshadow anything produced in the past.

For instance, internal adjustments, coated and fogproof lenses and compact design are standard on most models, but that's just the beginning. Beyond that are features that provide the shooter all kinds of special advantages. One of the most significant is the variable scope that can change magnification with the twist of a dial. A variety of choices exists, with the 1.5×-6×, 2×-7×, 3×-9×

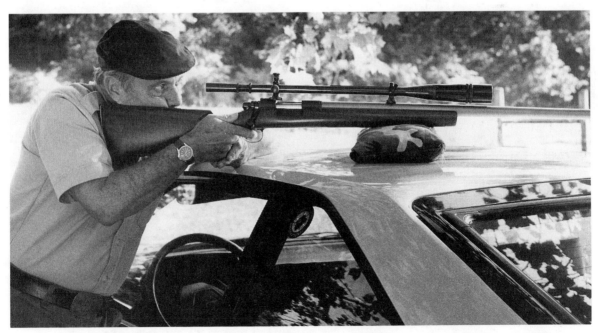

Firing the Remington 40XB in the field using a sandbag on a car top as a rest.

There are many high-quality rifle scopes on the market; the most popular are those with a variable power range.

the most popular, but 6×-24× models are also available for ultra-long-range shooting. Too, there are scopes with built-in rangefinders and trajectory compensators that take some guesswork out of zeroing in on a target. And it's no

problem finding the kind of reticle that suits the best, since there are many from which to choose. If you like, you can also have a laser scope, or one with just a lighted dot.

As rifle scope technology improved, so did

The Bausch & Lomb Elite spotting scope on a window mount makes viewing territory easy for a roaming varmint hunter.

A Bushnell field tripod with a binocular adapter allows comfortable scanning with Bausch & Lomb's Elite 10×42 binoculars.

that devoted to spotting scopes and binoculars. Both are very important items on the range and in the field. They're made more versatile by window mounts for locating targets from the comfort of the car seat, and special brackets that permit mounting binoculars on a tripod make it much more comfortable to scan with the higher-power glasses.

Yet, although rifle scopes offer shooters a definite advantage, the real test of marksmanship still lies with the individual. Simply attaching one to a rifle doesn't assure an instant improvement in shooting skills. A lot more is involved, and while no single formula works in all situations, there is a basic plan to follow.

SIGHTING IN

Place the rifle on a sandbag or other solid rest with the target 50 yards away. Bore-sighting will help put the first shot on paper. Next, by manipulating the vertical and horizontal adjustments, a few more shots should bring the point of impact to the desired place. Follow this with a 100-yard test using a target with the appropriate-sized bullseye. By checking the ballistic information for the cartridge, it can be determined where the bullet should be striking at 100, 200 or more yards, according to range capability. Of course, this will apply only to the cartridge being used, and a change in any of its characteristics—powder charge, bullet weight, and style—will alter the trajectory pattern. It's an early hint as to how many variables exist, and how complex things can become later.

The performance of a rifle depends on the skill of the person handling it. No matter how excellent the equipment, unless the shooter can place the crosshairs or dot precisely on the target and squeeze the trigger properly, it can serve no benefit.

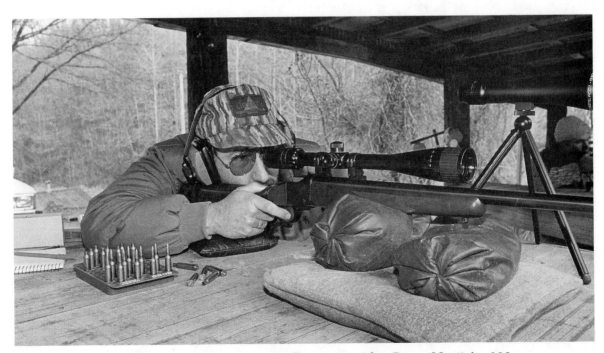

Shooting from the bench on sandbags rest with a Ruger No. 1 in .220 Swift; Bausch & Lomb 6×-24× scope; and Bausch & Lomb Elite spotting scope and Silencio ear protectors.

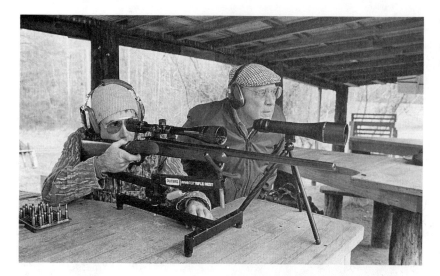

This benchrest shooter supports his rifle on an Outers Varminter rifle rest.

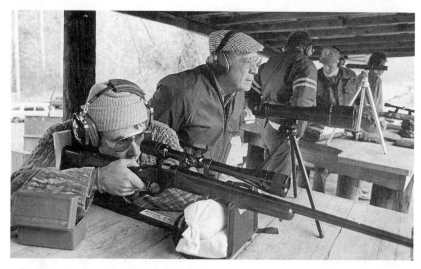

Here a shooter supports his rifle on a Tenex Recoil-A-Rest-R.

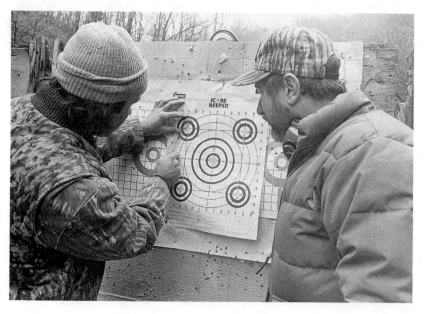

Hunters measure groups on a 200-yard target.

CLEANING A RIFLE

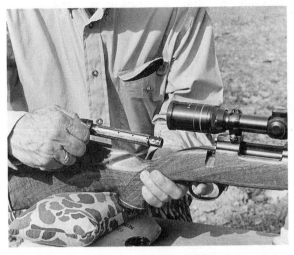

1. First step is removal of the bolt.

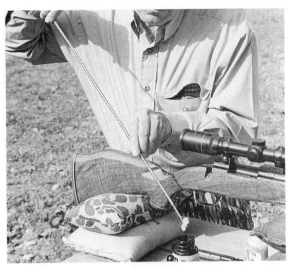

2. Since lead and copper accumulate in the barrel, it's necessary to use a good solvent.

3. Run the patch through the barrel several times to be certain that all of the residue is wiped away.

Pistols need the same care as rifles. This Harris Bipod supports pistol for cleaning.

Rusty Duck cleaning kit has everything needed for cleaning guns in the field.

This handy Kleen Bore cleaning kit is pocket sized.

An assortment of cleaning kits, including a couple of deluxe models.

CLEANLINESS

Equally as vital to precision shooting is keeping the rifle or handgun bore and mechanism spotlessly clean. In many cases, according to the loads being used, it's necessary to run a swab through the bore after every few shots. Lead and copper accumulations in the barrel have a very significant effect on bullet performance, and a full complement of cleaning equipment is a must on the range. The same applies for shooting in the field when a lot of rounds are going

to be fired. There are cleaning kits designed for every situation and circumstance that range from pocket size to large, deluxe models. By comparison with the older solvents and lubricants, modern products make gun cleaning a pleasure, and they are much more effective in keeping the equipment in top shape.

For those wishing to delve deeper into the subject of varmint rifles, no better source is available than Jim Carmichel's *Book of the Rifle*, which is recognized as the standard reference on the subject.

5

Woodchucks

Today's varmint hunters owe a great debt of gratitude to the woodchuck, or groundhog, because it is the animal on which the sport of varmint hunting was founded. Since the "pest guns" of the early days, the woodchuck has been what could be termed the official unit of measure for cartridge and rifle development. It is also what helped to define this type of hunting as a distinct and separate shooting sport and to elevate it to its present sophisticated and high-tech status. Today it remains the most popular of all varmints, and despite all of the attention it has received over the years, still one of the most abundant.

The woodchuck is another of the rodents in the Sciuridae family that includes about five dozen species in areas from the Arctic to Mexico, and although its range isn't that broad, it still occupies a lot of territory. Woodchucks are found all across Canada and into east-central Alaska, and southward into northern Idaho. In the rest of the United States, they occur from northeastern North Dakota south to Arkansas, and from New England to western North and South Carolina and northern Georgia and Alabama.

There is only one woodchuck species, but due to the color variations that occur in the different locations they inhabit, they're called by other names. In the high mountains of the West, woodchucks are known as whistlers or yellowbelly marmots, the latter of which is a separate species. They also have local nicknames such as "pasture pigs" or "pasture poodles."

The extent of their range also indicates the versatility of the animal in adapting to a wide variety of conditions from sea level to high altitudes, and from southern climes to the deep-freeze temperatures of the Far North. The same goes for habitat. Although most woodchuck hunting is done on farmlands, they also are found in non-farming areas. They're just as much at home on mountain slopes, in woods, and along streams or rivers, although in these places the population levels are lower than where crops are grown.

Woodchucks are heavy-bodied, short-legged animals that may attain weights of up to 14 pounds. Their fur varies from a yellowish brown to almost black, and is grizzled with white-tipped hairs. The undersides are a much lighter color. They are burrowers, using their

Woodchuck

about even in the snow. Usually this is because their sleeping chamber wasn't excavated deep enough below the frost line to keep them warm, or their body fat wasn't sufficient to maintain body heat. Such animals seldom survive.

In the South, though, woodchucks remain only semi-dormant and are likely to emerge anytime there's a warming trend. Since states in this latitude don't have winter-long snow cover, some kinds of food are always available for the off-season snackers.

This animal is best known to the general public for its habit of hibernation. This is because of an old European legend that claims that if on February 2 (Groundhog Day) the woodchuck emerges and sees its shadow, there will be six more weeks of winter. This superstition is said to have been introduced here by immigrants who settled in the South. However, the focus of attention on this make-believe, scheduled appearance has long been captured by the town of Punxsutawney, Pennsylvania, where the ritual is staged with a pet animal, "Punxsutawney Phil," and gets plenty of media exposure each year.

The woodchuck is mostly a vegetarian which feeds on grasses, clover, alfalfa and other succulent plants, although it will also eat insects, small birds and mice. It has a great fondness for grain crops, and the damage several of these animals can do to a field of young corn and soybean plants can make it appear that areas have been mowed. In places near cities where much truck farming is conducted, woodchucks invade fields and enthusiastically go after cabbage, lettuce, cauliflower, beans, peas and root vegetables. Even a few animals can make heavy inroads into these crops in a short time, so they're classed as major pests by the farmers. They can create similar havoc in domestic gardens.

Before most of the large timber tracts in the eastern United States were cut, the populations of these animals were minimal. Once agricultural practices were begun and an abundance of

forelegs to loosen the soil, and kicking it out with their hind legs. Generally solitary, about the only time two adults are together is during the mating period. The young are born in late April or May, with from four to six in a litter, and the female is entirely in charge of rearing them. At about two months of age they disperse and are on their own.

The dens woodchucks create typically have several entrances, with tunnels 30 to 40 feet in length and sometimes extending to depths of 30 or more feet. Centrally located in the network of tunnels is a large chamber that contains a grassy nest. There will also be chambers for food storage, and for defecation, the latter being sealed off once full.

Woodchucks almost always hibernate during the entire winter in the northern part of their range, but sometimes they are seen moving food became available, their numbers increased dramatically. Due to this environmental change, there are likely more of them present today than when the Pilgrims arrived.

The woodchuck is also responsible for livestock injuries. Cattle and sheep can suffer broken legs by stepping into their den entrances, and while the instances of this may be very infrequent, the possibility of it happening is enough to encourage landowners to get rid of the rodents. A real threat is having the ground above heavily tunneled areas collapse under the weight of tractors or other heavy farm machin-

ery and causing broken axles or other costly mechanical damage. Also, in places where concentrations of woodchuck burrows occur, they can cause sinkholes to develop.

A woodchuck's home range is usually between fifty and a hundred acres, depending on the kind of territory they occupy. In locations away from agricultural activities, they often wander over larger areas in order to find sufficient food. In order to assure their safety on their longer trips, they develop a series of alternate dens that can be used for emergency purposes, whether it be a threat or bad weather.

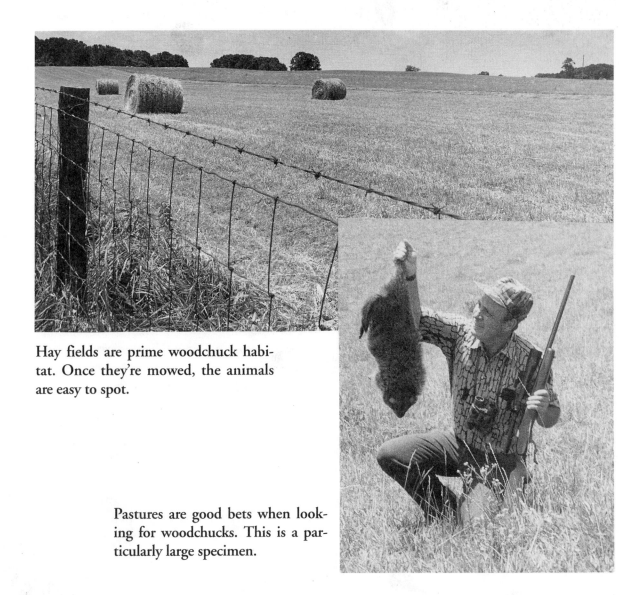

Hay fields are prime woodchuck habitat. Once they're mowed, the animals are easy to spot.

Pastures are good bets when looking for woodchucks. This is a particularly large specimen.

However, woodchucks generally don't settle in at any place that doesn't have a fairly generous food supply within a short distance of their dens. If this should dwindle for some reason, they will move on.

While woodchucks spend the principal amount of their time either on the ground or under it, they can climb trees with considerable dexterity; and despite their stubby legs, they're quite good swimmers. When gathering food, they can carry fairly large amounts in their pouched cheeks, dashing back to their dens every now and then to deposit the booty. Most of the activity occurs in the early morning and late afternoon hours. During the heat of midday, they usually loaf in the cool confines of their burrows.

In extremely hot weather, woodchucks may virtually disappear. These "siestas" may last for as long as several weeks, during which time hunters are better off staying at home near the air conditioner watching baseball games. When cooler early-autumn weather finally arrives, woodchucks finally emerge and begin a feeding binge that will add the layers of fat needed to sustain them through the coming winter. This increased activity makes the fall months especially productive for hunters, and it's usually the best time of the year to be in the field. The animals are also engaged in another important activity: preparing their dens for the long winter ahead. If the one they're occupying isn't just right, they either renovate it or go to work on digging another that will be suitable.

Man is the most important enemy of the woodchuck, but they're also preyed upon by coyotes and foxes. Hawks can't handle anything but young woodchucks, which don't come out of the den often; and when they do, they are kept close to the entrance by the mother. In places where there are eagles, these birds are capable of snatching up full-grown animals. Too, since woodchucks often like to feed alongside highways, many fall victim to vehicles.

Not many hunters eat woodchucks. They're missing an enjoyable experience. The meat is very tasty, and properly prepared can be as desirable as most small-game animals. Predictably, young ones are the best.

The other foes of woodchucks are mainly fleas and ticks, both of which are capable of creating infestations severe enough to either drive the animals from their dens or cause them to become too weak to survive.

Although the focus of attention is mainly on the economic downside of the woodchuck, its lifestyle also has benefits. The burrows they create become dens for other animals, including cottontail rabbits, skunks, opossums, foxes and raccoons. At one time woodchucks were protected by law in Pennsylvania because their burrows served as havens for rabbits during the winter. Rabbits were prime game for hunters, and the state was interested in their survival because of the license revenue it collected. The law was eventually rescinded, and today Pennsylvania may actually have more woodchuck hunters than any other state in the nation.

Getting permission from landowners to hunt woodchucks seldom is any problem, mainly because unlike game animals, these are critters they *want* to be rid of. They consider that the varmint hunter is doing them a favor, saving them both time and trouble. As long as a hunter conducts himself properly, there's usually a standing invitation for return visits. Good relationships are valuable, and as a hunter explores more territory and becomes acquainted with more farmers and landowners, more places become available to shoot woodchucks. It's smart to have plenty of "aces in the hole," just in case!

Hunters in the West are outside the woodchuck's range, but an animal that's quite similar in appearance and habit provides plenty of action for them.

The **Yellowbelly Marmot**, or rockchuck, is a smaller version of the woodchuck, with brownish-yellow upperparts, a yellow belly, light to dark brown feet and a pair of white spots between its eyes. It weighs between 5 and 10 pounds.

The yellowbelly marmot's diet includes grasses, succulent plants and berries. Although it is a burrower, sometimes the dens are found in rock crevices, rock shelters, and under rock piles. These animals form colonies and inhabit mostly mountain regions up to elevations of 12,000 feet. They enter into hibernation at different times, disappearing as early as August in some locations. Emergence is usually in early spring, and mating takes place shortly afterward.

Their range includes British Columbia, Alberta, Washington, Oregon, California, Idaho, Montana, Wyoming, Utah and Colorado. It's important to know that this animal is host to the tick that carries Rocky Mountain spotted fever.

Another species, the **Hoary Marmot**, also has the nickname rockchuck, but its range is mainly in British Columbia, Alaska and the Yukon, with some found in the high country of northern Washington, Idaho and Montana.

This burrower is quite different in appearance from the yellowbelly species. It is slightly larger, attaining weights of up to 20 pounds, and has a silver-gray upper body and a whitish belly. There are distinctive white and black spots on its head.

Because of the remote areas most of the hoary marmots inhabit, they aren't seriously sought by varmint hunters, but Indians of the region use their pelts for parkas, and also like to eat them. Their other enemies are wolves, bears and eagles. There are several subspecies, none of which are of significance to hunters.

HUNTING METHODS

Woodchucks are not only found in a wide diversity of habitat, they are hunted in a variety of ways. Compare the farm youth prowling pastures with a .22 rifle, looking for a 50-yard shot, to the fellow with a .220 Swift with a 6×-24× scope zeroed in on a target too distant to see clearly with the naked eye.

In between lies a broad array of weapons and hunting tactics.

Terrain has much to do with the choice of guns and methods. There's a big difference

Yellowbelly Marmot

between shooting over flat farmlands and hilly country, at animals in secluded woods or in spots close to human habitation. A proficient hunter will be capable of handling these challenges.

The woodchuck has always been associated with long-range, precision shooting. The hunter seeks out groundhog habitat, scouts it thoroughly, then returns to set up at a place where the territory can be observed with binoculars and spotting scopes at whatever distance desired from the burrow openings. Usually, the location selected will provide the chance to bag several animals, and the hunt may be an all-day affair.

This is a situation where the best of equipment and accessories can be put to test. Ideally, conditions approximating or duplicating benchrest shooting can be achieved: distances can be accurately measured and point of bullet impact observed.

There's nothing rudimentary about such setups, and in many instances the major objective is not to bag woodchucks but to experiment with bullet capabilities and performance. That's how the sport began, and this aspect of it has never changed. Of course these shooter/technicians have contributed immensely in the development of the varmint-hunting tools available today, and they continue to do so.

There are field shooters who don't go to such extremes, but the method is somewhat similar. Once a woodchuck-laden field is found, they pick a good spot and wait for the action to begin. One of the best ways to find places with plenty of animals is to drive around back roads and stop to glass every pasture or open field. Sometimes the animals don't have to be visible, since groundhog holes are easy to spot from a distance.

The best times to scout are in the morning before the sun gets too high, or from mid to late afternoon. Spend some time finding places where there's lots of activity. You'll develop an inventory of dependable spots to visit. Once permission to hunt at each is obtained, there's no problem in finding action.

No matter what the hunting methods, keep a record of each excursion. Note the date, time of day, weather conditions, ground cover (crops, pasture, etc.) and number of animals taken; the data will be useful in planning future trips. All are important factors to be considered when developing hunt plans.

The "walk around" approach, in which the hunter sets out on foot to locate the quarry, is probably the most challenging method. A lot of different skills are required to be successful. This is a hunting style that works well in undulating or rough terrain which can't be surveyed from a distance. It's a slow, deliberate kind of stalking. You have to stop frequently and scan the terrain, trying to spot a woodchuck before it sees you, then sneak up as close as possible before shooting.

Sometimes this is a fairly easy matter, but there are instances when some extra effort and caution must be exerted. A good example of this is trying to bag woodchucks in soybean fields when the plants are about 18 inches high. Groundhogs can't be seen when on all fours in feeding position, but every now and then they stand up to check for danger. Once you determine an animal's location, you can belly-crawl between the rows until close enough for a sure off-hand shot. It's best to be at least three rows to either side of the one in which the woodchuck is foraging. It's a game of chance in some respects, because the time comes when you have to rise for a peek, and if the woodchuck does the same thing simultaneously, you'll miss the opportunity. This is a tactic that also pays off well for blackpowder enthusiasts, bowhunters and handgunners.

One of the most overlooked methods is what might be termed ultra-*close* shooting. This entails eradicating the varmints around, and sometimes in, farm buildings, particularly ones in which hay or grain are stored. However, no structures are exempted as possible home sites, including residences.

The extent of damage done by the animals in

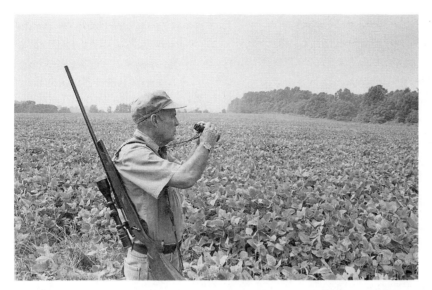

Woodchucks are not hard to spot in soybean fields when the plants are still fairly short. After that, they can move about and not be detected.

The light Weatherby .224 Magnum is perfect for off-hand shooting.

such situations can be extensive. The most serious occurs when woodchuck burrows undermine foundations, which can cause all or parts of the building to collapse. Too, living in close proximity to the farmer's garden, they can have a significant impact in that respect. One woodchuck can inflict more harm on a vegetable plot than several rabbits.

This is a pestilence far more common than realized, and it offers an excellent opportunity to engage in a new tactic while performing a valuable service to the landowner. However, few hunters are aware of this opportunity, and most farmers think hunters are interested only in long-range shooting. All it takes to get a crack at these close-in groundhogs is to ask your host if he has such a problem. If so, you can bet on an invitation to be an exterminator!

This is a perfect situation for some cartridges that no longer enjoy high-profile status. The venerable .22 Hornet is one, since it's efficient and is less noisy than some of the hotter loads. Some other good choices are the .17 Rem., .218 Bee, .25/20 Win. and .32/20 Win. Since shots

One reason farmers dislike woodchucks is that their burrows often cause damage to livestock and farm machinery.

Woodchucks like to burrow under farmhouses and outbuildings, even abandoned residences like this.

are at close range, this circumstance is also suitable for the .22 Mag and for handguns and archery equipment.

These down-home woodchucks pose a challenge, since they frequently are very wary, having been harassed by dogs and sometimes peppered with shot by the farmer. It takes stealth and patience to score, and if several are present, things get tougher after the first one is bagged.

Something that was mentioned before: woodchucks are just as likely to be found under and around abandoned buildings and under old

Fencerows can be productive for woodchucks, since they often locate their burrows in the cover that grows up alongside them.

Sometimes woodchuck dens are so well hidden in the cover along fencerows that the animals are difficult to spot.

A fence post makes a good rest for the scope-sighted Thompson/Center carbine in .17 Remington.

farm machinery that has been left in the field with vegetation growing up around it.

Sinkholes are places that almost always have woodchuck populations. They're perfect havens, undisturbed by agricultural practices but in close proximity to the crops. The key to success in hunting these places is to scout them in advance and locate the burrows to determine the best angle of approach.

Woodchucks like to make burrows in places that offer safety and easy access to food sources. Sinkholes are only one of the places that provide both. There are several others that are equally attractive.

Fencerows or hedgerows have special appeal, since they are avenues between croplands that provide both cover and travel lanes. Burrows can't be disturbed by plowing or harvesting, yet food sources are literally right at their front doors. In areas where there are rock walls, the same applies.

The way to hunt these sites is to first glass both sides and see if any burrows or animals are visible. If nothing shows, then begin a quiet stalk along the side that you judge to be the most favorable for a stalk. Stop frequently and continue to keep glassing on the area ahead, as well as whatever can be seen on the opposite side. Very often, if you're quiet enough, it's possible to walk within a few yards of a groundhog sunning itself at the burrow's entrance.

Small woodlots are also frequently inhabited by woodchucks, but locating the burrows can be difficult, and it's equally hard to hunt them in these places. However, if they're known to be present, by sitting at the woods' edge and waiting, there's a chance to get a crack at them as they travel to and from feeding areas.

There's no better way to cover a lot of territory and get in plenty of shooting than by walking railroad tracks, a point of access to hunting territory described earlier in the chapter on squirrels. The embankments along the roadbeds have always been prime places for woodchuck burrows, and like some of the spots just described, they're near or adjacent to croplands. Stalking from the tracks is a quiet approach, and very efficient, since often the hunter is in an elevated position with excellent short- and long-range visibility.

Topographical maps can be useful in checking out local potential for this kind of hunting, because they show the locations where the tracks pass through the most farmland. You can select a few sections that look good and make trial runs. Eventually, you'll accumulate a list of those that are the most productive.

One of the benefits of this type of tactic is that it can double your opportunity. For instance, if you walk a couple miles of track, the return trip provides nearly the same amount of potential. Any animals disturbed will have overcome their caution and again be active. Many railroads have ceased to operate, but their tracks or roadbeds are still intact, so these "avenues" remain available to varmint hunters.

Another challenging hunting tactic is to float rivers that run through woodchuck habitat. This is a totally silent and effortless way to stalk, and it gives access to some extremely productive habitat. Streamside tree lines serve not only as buffers between cultivated fields but also as ideal places for groundhogs to settle in. A particular advantage is that green vegetation can be found near water the year around in most places, providing food for the animals at times when other foods aren't readily available

Canoes or kayaks have traditionally been the most popular means of conveyance, but in recent years some very sophisticated float tubes have been produced. One of the advantages floating offers is access to territory normally not invaded by varmint hunters.

Floating is one of the few methods of woodchuck hunting where shotguns are sometime used. Canoes, kayaks and float tubes are relatively unstable shooting platforms from which it is difficult to shoot accurately. Shotguns with

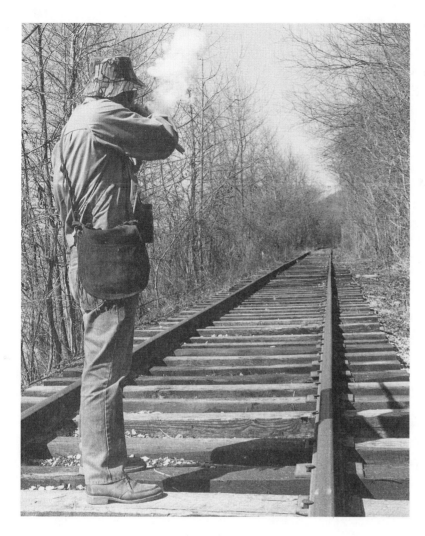

Walking along railroad tracks is a good way to hunt woodchucks, since they often make their dens along the adjacent embankments.

large buckshot get good results at distances up to fifty yards.

One of the most interesting and challenging places to hunt woodchucks is in mountainous regions like the southern Appalachians. There are vastly more animals in the highlands than might be imagined, yet pursuing them requires considerably different techniques and a lot more physical stamina than most other forms of the sport. Conversely, it can bring out the best in both hunter and quarry.

With few, if any, agricultural crops upon which to depend for subsistence, the high-country chucks do more diversified foraging than their lowland cousins. Because of this, their feeding patterns are less predictable. Burrow openings are what mountain hunters look for.

The best friend a varmint hunter can have in getting into good mountain groundhog range is a four-wheel-drive vehicle, because much of it is at places where walking in is the only alternative. Even then, some additional foot travel is usually necessary.

The first rule in identifying the spots with the best promise is to determine which hillsides face east. Groundhogs prefer locations that receive morning sunlight, and in the mountains the western slopes remain in shade until the sun is high in the sky. Early light permits groundhogs to begin foraging while it's still cool, and once this is completed, they can spend time sunning at the entrances to their dens.

Hunting mountain wood-
chucks is challenging and
tough going at times.

The highlands afford the opportunity for both long- and short-range shooting. It's sometimes possible to set up on top of a ridge and shoot at woodchucks on the sides of adjacent hills. This kind of setting is one preferred by a clan of Pennsylvania varmint hunters who specialize in the ultimate in extended range shooting. These individuals use custom rifles chambered for .50 caliber cartridges necked down to smaller calibers, even as far as sabotted .17 Remington, and military-type range-finding equipment. With the heavier bullets, shots as distant as 1,000 yards can be made; but lighter bullets, such as in the .17 Remington, can't hold up at extremely long ranges. This style of varminting isn't likely ever to enjoy great popularity, but it does indicate that there are always people exploring the outer limits of the sport.

A more strenuous approach to hunting high-country woodchucks is to tackle the hilly terrain on foot. The animals will be either above or below your line of travel, and bagging them is more like sniping than anything else. It's also tricky, because as every rifleman knows, steep angle shots increase the chances of a miss. This danger is magnified even more when shooting is done offhand: you're walking along, spot a groundhog and have to fire before it dives into its hole.

Mountain groundhogs have the advantage when hunters approach from below. They have good visibility and their attention is usually focused downhill. The odds change when the positions are reversed and the hunter is on top looking down, which is a sound reason for walking along the crests of hills rather than in the valleys.

Hunting from vehicles is popular, and it's a very effective way to bag woodchucks. This gives the hunter great mobility and a stable shooting platform. Driving to the edge of a large field or pasture in a pickup truck and setting up the spotting scope, sandbags and other accessories on the roof provides a close approximation of benchrest shooting. Shooters who use cars equip them with window mounts for both spotting scopes and rifles and get similar stability. Shooting off the hood is widely practiced, too.

The laws on the use of vehicles for varmint hunting vary considerably from state to state. Some forbid it entirely, while others permit it on some types of roads. Some permit hunting from vehicles on private land and away from public roads. And it's worth mentioning that in some instances there's a distinction made

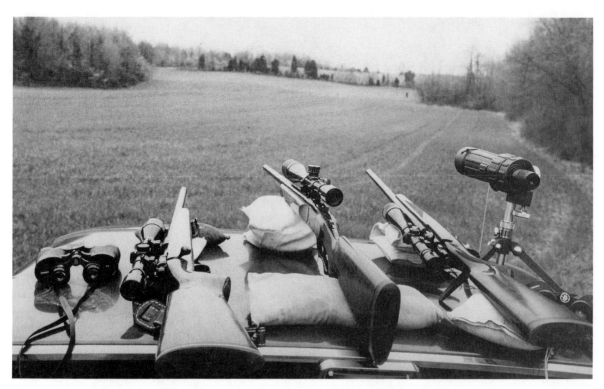

The top of a pickup truck makes an ideal shooting platform that provides extra elevation.

between firing out the windows and from outside the vehicle.

There are other advantages to using a vehicle besides convenience. Woodchucks are accustomed to seeing farm machinery, so approaching or entering a field in a car or truck isn't likely to cause the animals any concern. To the contrary, it often allows hunters to get much closer than would otherwise be possible. A second plus applies particularly to pickup trucks, which provide elevation and enable the shooter to see animals that wouldn't be visible from ground level due to cover or undulations in the terrain.

Aside from cars and trucks, there's good utility for the four-wheel all-terrain vehicles that are popular for many other kinds of hunting. Because of their versatility, they give varmint hunters extended range beyond that of conventional vehicles. Equipped with racks for holding guns and storing gear, they are much like magic

carpets on which to cover country that would ordinarily have to be traveled on foot.

EQUIPMENT AND ACCESSORIES

Obviously, the right weapon is the most vital piece of equipment. Any of the varmint rifles discussed in the preceding chapter are suitable. Handguns are becoming increasingly popular with woodchuck hunters, for both short- and long-range shooting. The Remington XP-100 and Thompson/Center Contender are favorites, and both are available in a wide variety of varmint cartridges. Equipped with a good scope and in the hands of an experienced shooter, these are very accurate at ranges up to 200 yards. When woodchucks can be stalked and approached to within 50 yards of less, using big-bore pistols with open sights offers handgunners a special challenge. It's a good way to

Lots of woodchuck hunters like to use handguns, and no holds are barred in regard to caliber. Shown here, clockwise from bottom left: Iver Johnson .22 automatic; Thompson/Center Contender with JDJ Special .45-70 barrel, Simmons scope and Harris Bipod; Remington XP-100 Varminter in .223 with Leupold scope; Ruger Red Hawk in .44 Magnum; Ruger Black Hawk Single Six in .357 Magnum.

Taking aim at a woodchuck with the Remington XP-100 from a reclining position.

get in some practice that's more fun than shooting on a standard range.

Speaking of the big boomers, woodchucks also offer hunters the chance to shoot large-caliber rifles that are normally intended for use on game as large as elephants and are chambered for such cartridges as the .375 H&H Magnum, .340 Weatherby Magnum, .416 Rigby, .458 Winchester Magnum and .470 Nitro Express. Accuracy with these big rifles can be improved significantly by shooting in the field rather than on the range.

Woodchucks give hunters the opportunity to use big-bore rifles. This custom A-Square .416 Rigby can down an elephant.

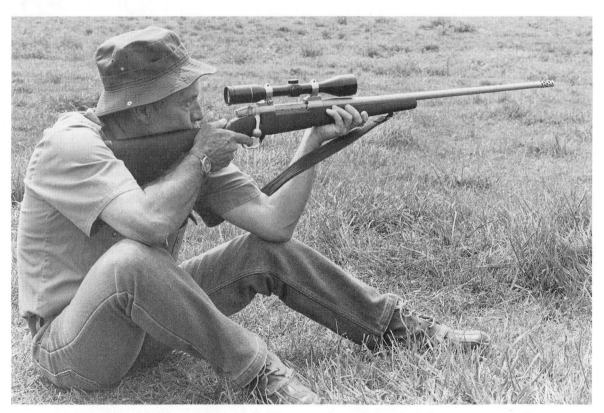

The Weatherby Alaskan in .340 Weatherby Magnum has a recoil arrestor and a good recoil pad, so it's not unpleasant to shoot.

Optics are needed for hunting woodchucks. This shooter is equipped with a rifle and a spotting scope.

Next in importance is having the right kind of optics. The ability to locate game, get a precise look at it, and then place bullets accurately at distant targets is dependent upon binoculars, spotting scopes and telescope sights. Without these, the sport of varmint hunting would be restricted to only short- range shooting with iron sights.

A good rifle scope stands as the top priority. A 4× scope is suitable for short ranges, while targets at 200 yards or more require much higher magnification to achieve precise bullet placement. A hunter can choose from fixed or variable-power models with power ranges up to 24×. Due to a highly competitive market, good-quality scopes can be bought at reasonable prices, but those designed for ultra-long-range or target shooting are expensive.

No hunter should be without a set of good binoculars, because they serve many purposes. Spotting game is one, but they are also very helpful in looking over terrain and developing strategies. Technological advances have made it possible for manufacturers to produce light, compact models of excellent quality that can be carried in a shirt or jacket pocket. However, many hunters prefer larger binoculars with higher magnification and a greater field of view.

Although binoculars are fine for spotting game, spotting scopes with very high magnification make it possible to examine the target closely, determine the best time to shoot and have an instant view of the results. Scopes were once used mainly by hunters shooting from fixed positions, but now several lightweight models are available that are suitable for backpacking.

Rangefinders can be of great help in determining shooting distances. Several models are

A good rangefinder can measure distances with great precision, making it possible to zero in accurately on the target.

The Harris Bipod extends so a shooter can fire from a sitting position, an advantage in tall grass. It provides excellent stability.

available from Ranging that can gauge ranges up to 1,000 yards and are extremely accurate.

Hunters who don't own one or more Harris bipods are usually those who haven't used one of these devices. The great stability they provide aids immensely in precise bullet placement at long ranges. The bipods attach to the forend of the rifle and fold away when not in use, and they are equally as good as a sandbag for support. There are several models, one which extends to permit shooting from a sitting position, a valuable advantage in tall grass.

Since woodchuck hunters get a lot of exposure to the summer elements, using a high number sun block, sunglasses and wearing a broad-brimmed hat can help ward off skin and eye problems. Insect repellants are useful items to have along, particularly those that ward off ticks, chiggers and mosquitoes. Lying on the ground or walking through grass and other vegetation almost always results in encounters with some of these pests.

Another item that's highly practical is a small tarp or ground cloth to use in early morning when the dew is still on the grass, or when recent rains have left the earth soggy. Accessories can be spread out and organized better on a ground cloth.

For hunters who will be moving around, all of these accessories can be easily carried in a day pack, along with lunch, a canteen of water and a light rain jacket or poncho.

6

Prairie Dogs

Some animals end up with names that are only half right. The sea lion is an example, for while it lives in the ocean, it isn't a feline. The "lion" part results from its similar roar.

The same is true of the prairie dog, which indeed inhabits the region the name suggests, but it isn't a canine. It does "bark," if that's how one chooses to interpret the sound it makes.

Two early French explorers, Louis and Francois Verendrye, who were roaming what is now Canada in the mid-1700s, swung southward into the region that was later to become North and South Dakota and Montana. In the process, they came upon huge colonies of small ground-dwelling animals that sat up, picket-like, on their den mounds and vocally protested the explorers' presence with high-pitched yips. The Verendryes promptly labeled them *petit chien*, which means "little dog."

That took care of half of the name. The "prairie" prefix was added in 1804 by Meriwether Lewis. Leading the Lewis and Clark expedition through this same region, he noticed that the little animals were found mostly in the prairies. Apparently he was aware of the title given them by the earlier explorers and chose not to alter the "dog" part. Scientific accuracy in classifying new animals wasn't closely observed in those days, which is why we have several other misnamed species, examples of which are elk, antelope and buffalo.

The prairie dog is another member of the squirrel family, and certainly the darling of varmint hunters in the areas it inhabits. No other animal is as numerous or as prolific, so there's never any problem finding action in prairie dog country when weather and seasonal conditions are right. In effect, it's the western version of the woodchuck—and then some!

There are four species, **Black-tailed Prairie Dog**, **White-tailed Prairie Dog**, **Gunnison's Prairie Dog**, and **Utah Prairie Dog**, but the first two are the ones that attract almost all of the varmint hunter's attention. The Gunnison's occu-

Prairie Dog

pies a much smaller range and is less numerous, and the Utah is classed as endangered.

The white-tailed prairie dog is the species with the widest distribution. Before the Great Plains were settled, its range extended from Saskatchewan to the Rio Grande. Within this territory were gigantic dog towns, and there are some early accounts of their size that are truly amazing. One of these, written in 1852 by R.B. Marcy, told of a one-million-acre tract that had an estimated five million inhabitants. At about the same time, John R. Bartlett reported that he had ridden on horseback for three days along a tributary of the Colorado River in Texas without getting outside the limits of one mammoth and continuous prairie dog community.

Later descriptions of prairie dog populations in particular areas include one by a biologist, Hart Merriam, who in 1900 spent several weeks studying a town near San Angelo, Texas that was 250 miles long and 100 miles wide. His conclusion was that there were at least four million animals inhabiting it. In 1931, Vernon Bailey claimed that 6,400,000 was a conservative estimate of the prairie dog population of Grant County, New Mexico. And even as late as 1945,

Bert Popowski said he saw a dog town in northern Nebraska that paralleled a railroad track for 20 miles.

Today, the majority of large prairie dog villages are on protected lands, and both their range and numbers have been much reduced from pioneer times. Presently, the black-tailed is found from eastern Montana and southwest North Dakota to northwest Texas, New Mexico and a small part of southeastern Arizona. The white-tailed is a resident of a much smaller pocket of territory that includes southeastern Utah, southwestern Colorado, northeast Arizona and northwest New Mexico.

The settlement of the Great Plains and the subsequent agricultural development of the land substantially reduced the prairie dog population. Farmers and ranchers believed that prairie dogs were in conflict with their interests, so they initiated mass extermination projects. Poison was the main instrument of destruction. A spoonful of grain soaked with strychnine poured into each burrow opening assured death to all of its inhabitants. Traps were also used, as well as gas, and everyone with a rifle was eager to plink away at prairie dogs.

The campaigns to wipe out prairie dogs lasted for many years. With the reduction of available habitat owing to the increase in human population and land development, no comeback was possible.

Fortunately, the pressure was gradually reduced as it became apparent that these animals weren't as detrimental to human efforts as was first believed. They were initially charged with eating grass ranchers needed to fatten cattle, and while this is true, it isn't their main source of food. Prairie dogs eat many weeds and plants that cattle ignore. There was also the claim that their burrow openings were responsible for breaking the legs of livestock. This may occur to a small extent, but looking at it from a different perspective, the burrowing serves to rejuvenate the soil, and abandoned dens are

often occupied by various creatures including owls and rabbits, various other small rodents, salamanders, lizards and snakes.

Today landowners are more tolerant of prairie dogs, as long as their numbers don't become excessive. This attitude usually provides an opening and often a warm welcome for varmint hunters, and there's no shortage of opportunities for all-day shoots in the areas where they're still abundant. Given the present circumstances, there's every reason to believe that this sport will continue to be available to shooters in the future.

BLACK-TAILED PRAIRIE DOG

Because of its wide range and great numbers, the black-tailed prairie dog is the best-known and most sought of the two major species. It is also the largest, weighing from 2 to 3 pounds. The upper body is a pinkish-brown, with off-white underparts. Its tail is slim, sparsely haired and black-tipped. The ears are small and rounded, and the eyes black. The favored habitat is shortgrass prairies.

Prairie dogs are primarily herbivorous, and their diet consists almost entirely of green plants, most of which are the kinds of grasses that are available in any particular area. They favor bluegrass, brome grass, gramagrass, burro grass and purple needle grass, but they will also vary this with grasshoppers and other insects. There is seldom any kind of vegetation in the vicinity of their burrows. They eat this first, so there is no way predators can approach without being seen.

On hot summer days, prairie dogs feed in the early morning and late afternoon and sleep during the midday heat. In cooler weather the animals may be active all through the day, although they won't remain above ground during storms. Black-tails seldom venture very far from their burrows, since they are vulnerable once distant from these havens.

The burrows display an instinctive sense of

A family of black-tailed prairie dogs gathered around their den.

engineering. Conical, well-tamped-down mounds at the entrance serve several purposes, one of which is to create a wall that prevents the burrow from being flooded during rainy weather. The top of the mound provides an elevated observation post, and by varying the height of the mound, the flow of air through the burrow can be regulated.

There are two or more burrow openings, between which is a horizontal tunnel that may be as deep as 14 feet below the surface with several chambers lined with grass that serve as nurseries and another for excrement. Like cats, prairie dogs cover their scat, and when a chamber is filled, it is sealed and another one excavated. Some food may be stored, but generally the animals depend on stored fat to tide them over during the winter, They do not hibernate, but during periods of severe cold or snowstorms they enter a lethargic state and sleep for a few days.

If a predator such as a snake enters one of the tunnels, the residents leave and quickly seal it off, sometimes at both ends, burying the intruder alive.

Just below the vertical shaft leading to the den's entrance is a short lateral tunnel that provides an out-of-sight listening post, and also a convenient place to turn around without descending into the main tunnel. Quite often, adjoining family groups have interlinking tunnels between the burrows.

Black-tails breed once a year, usually in February and March, and about a month later have a litter of four or five deaf, blind and hairless young. The offspring emerge into the daylight at about six weeks of age, then depart at about ten weeks. Full growth is achieved at six months. The average life span is seven or eight years.

Prairie dogs cooperate when building a town, but once this is accomplished, it is divided into several wards or neighborhoods. The occupants are friendly to one another, but moving from one neighborhood into another isn't tolerated. One characteristic prevalent among the black-tails is the habit of "kissing." Two animals approach each other and touch noses, then turn their heads to the side and touch incisors. Apparently this is for identifying ward and family members which work together building burrows. These same ward members groom each other.

In a dog town there are always sentinels on the alert. When danger threatens, one or more gives a sharp bark, and hundreds of animals simultaneously repeat the warning signal and dive into their burrows. Eventually, a few cautiously peek out to check the situation. If no threat is apparent, they give an all-clear signal called "yip-jump" display. The prairie dog leaps into the air while emitting a whistling yip, which is then repeated by others in the vicinity. The alarm cry and the all-clear sound are only two of nine distinctive calls that have been identified.

The black-tail has many predators, principal among which are badgers and foxes. Paradoxically, the extermination campaigns which wiped out 90 percent of the prairie dog population also decimated the numbers of what was then their chief predator, the black-footed ferret. Other enemies are coyotes, bobcats, hawks, owls, eagles, snakes, and, of course, humans. Modern techniques of modifying and improving habitat conditions, plus the effect of all of the predators, combine to maintain a balanced population. This has reduced the desire or need on the part of ranchers to eliminate them.

WHITE-TAILED PRAIRIE DOG

The white-tailed prairie dog is slightly smaller than its cousin, with upperparts that are a pinkish-buff mixed with black, and underparts that are slightly lighter. The tail is short and white-tipped. The ears are small and rounded, and there are distinctive dark patches above and below the eyes. The nose has a yellowish hue.

White-tails and black-tails inhabit different kinds of terrain. The white-tail occupies mountain regions to altitudes as high as 12,000 feet where conditions are dissimilar to those in the lowlands. White-tails form smaller colonies with few interlinking burrows, and "kissing" and mutual grooming aren't as prevalent.

White-tail burrows don't always have mounds. Often, excavated dirt is simply tossed to the side, and if it is built up slightly, it's seldom tamped down and washes away during a hard rain. Probably this lack of attention to the mound is because the white-tail doesn't require the clear view of its surroundings needed by the black-tail. For the same reason, they don't clear the vegetation in the vicinity of the den opening.

The mountaineers prefer much the same foods as the black-tails—grasses and a variety of other green plants—but their habitat may restrict their diet to mostly saltbush. Regardless of food choices, all prairie dogs gain weight rapidly during the summer months. A one-pound dog may be twice that heavy by the time fall arrives. In the case of the white-tail, this extra fat must carry them through the entire winter, since unlike the black-tails, they hibernate during the cold months. Usually, they go into this state by September, but some of the younger animals that haven't had this experience may remain active until October, trying to consume a full measure of "winter fuel."

Due to the difference in weather conditions, white-tails breed later than black-tails, usually in the latter part of March when temperatures at the higher elevations moderate sufficiently to make them active. The litters average five, and the young don't appear above ground until May or June. White-tails have a life expectancy of only four or five years.

The principal enemies of the white-tail are birds of prey, bobcats, badgers and coyotes, and there is a widespread, although unsubstantiated, belief that rattlesnakes take a great toll. Fire and floods kill a fairly large number each year. Man has greatly reduced the population of these animals by the use of poison, gas and traps. Much of this animosity against them has been significantly reduced, but high-country ranchers still welcome varmint hunters to keep their numbers at an acceptable level.

While it is unfortunate in some respects that the name "dog" was attached to this ground squirrel, native Americans regarded them as a diet staple, and it didn't take long for the early settlers to discover that the meat of these animals is quite palatable. There's no doubt that the prairie dog was more than once responsible for saving people from starvation, but more than that, it was a very acceptable source of protein on a regular basis. Apparently few if any of today's hunters have developed an appetite for them, but it's quite possible that some of the more curious and adventuresome individuals have given them a try. However, it's certain that their very name precludes the possibility that these animals will ever be accepted as table fare.

One serious problem that affects prairie dog towns is the occasional incidence of bubonic plague epidemics. The organism responsible for this deadly disease is transmitted by flea bites, and like almost all ground-dwelling members of the rodent order, prairie dogs are commonly victims of flea infestations. Public health officials monitor the dog towns for this hazard, and when it shows up, the sites are poisoned and flagged to alert hunters or others who might approach.

Oddly, this hasn't been a problem of any consequence in the woodchuck population, but this may be because these animals aren't by nature as colonial and closely congregated. No doubt they are susceptible, as any of the other rodents could be, but prairie dogs are the only ones which have demonstrated a propensity for such outbreaks.

There may be other problems lurking, though. As recently as 1992, the deaths of a number of Navajo Indians from a virus strain linked with the excretions of certain rodents has initiated investigations into the possibilities of danger that could be posed by a number of species that inhabit the same region.

This poses a dilemma. Although the prairie dog isn't on the endangered list, some of the other rodents are. Attempts at extermination will undoubtedly ignite more divisive people-versus-protected-species battles that have become commonplace in recent years.

HUNTING METHODS

All things considered, prairie dog hunting has no peer when it comes to fast action and plenty of targets. Even crow hunting can't compare. Where there is an abundance of animals, a hunter may fire as many as a thousand rounds in a day.

Some shooters consider hunting prairie dogs to be the most challenging, demanding and maddening of all varmint hunting sports.

For one thing, much of the range these animals occupy is flat and semiarid, hot and windy during the times when they are most active. In hot weather shimmering heat waves rise from the ground creating a mirage that makes a distant target wiggle like a hula dancer. The only way it can be avoided is by limiting hunting to the very early hours of the day. Also, high-velocity cartridges cause a barrel to become hot very rapidly. In extremely hot weather, the barrel must be allowed to cool between shots in order to avoid serious damage. If only one rifle is used, the action will necessarily be intermittent. For this reason, veteran dog hunters take several rifles along so they can switch around and keep on shooting. The favorite prairie dog rifle among many hunters who don't attempt ultra-long-range shooting is the .222 Remington, because it doesn't heat up quickly and can be used for longer periods of time than high-intensity cartridges. Some of the less potent, short-range .22s, both rimfire and centerfire, are useful to include in the arsenal for closer work.

Since most prairie dog hunters handload their ammunition and beef it up to their individual specifications, the rounds must be worked up at temperatures similar to those expected in the field. Heat causes changes in

Mirage can create problems for long-range rifles like this Ruger M77 Varmint in .223 with a Leupold 6.5×20 scope.

The Savage 112FV in .22-250 topped with a Simmons 6×20 scope is a good choice for prairie dogs.

pressure levels, and this factor must be taken into account in order to obtain precision performance. Factory loads aren't critical in this sense, so normal precautions of keeping ammunition out of direct sunlight is all that's required.

Wind is another factor, and it seems as if it blows more constantly in prairie dog country than anywhere else in America. A calm day is a rarity. "Reading the wind" is a skill that every hunter who shoots at long range yearns to perfect. In the case of prairie dog shooting with light bullets, the effects of air movement are especially pronounced.

There are numerous ways to determine wind direction and velocity. Tossing up bits of grass or a handful of dust is one, and looking at heat waves through binoculars or a rifle scope to see which direction they're leaning is another. Hanging a cotton ball on a string works well. There's also a manufactured device, available for a few dollars, that measures wind.

Veteran shooters rely primarily on experience and their own judgment to evaluate wind, and one thing that can be relied upon is to take a shot aimed dead on at the target and see where the bullet strikes. This will provide a pretty close indication of what's happening between you and whatever you're shooting at unless the

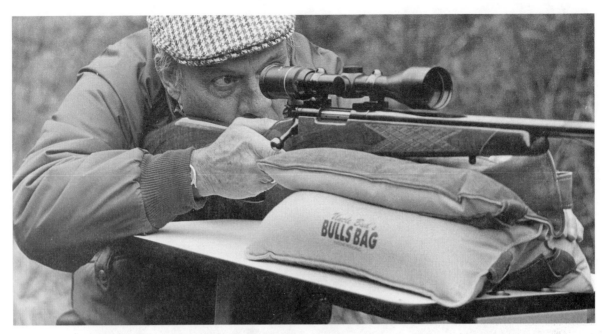

This heavy Bulls Bag on a portable shooting bench makes a solid rest for the shooter. The rifle is a Weatherby Mark V in .224 topped with a Weatherby 2×-7× scope.

wind is gusting. In this case, there simply isn't any way to assure accuracy.

Setting up for a prairie dog shoot near a dog town has many of the trappings of a tailgate party, because almost all of the conveniences of home can be brought along. The vehicle is driven to the spot where the shooting will be done, and all of the gear and accessories are unloaded and put into position. This usually includes a benchrest, sandbags, a spotting scope, binoculars, rangefinder, several rifles, a cleaning kit and plenty of ammunition. In the vehicle, which often is a van, there are refreshments, food, and best of all, shade and sometimes air conditioning. Conducted in this manner, it isn't a sport that creates hardships.

Of course, all hunters don't enjoy this kind

The Weatherby Mark V with a 2×–7× Supreme scope and a pair of Leupold Porro 10×40 binoculars are a nice combination for prairie dog hunting.

The Thompson/Center Carbine has interchangeable barrels, so a prairie dog hunter can use different cartridges. Also, when one barrel heats up, it's easy to switch to another.

of comfort, especially those who choose to walk around and take random shots at the animals at whatever distances they may happen to appear. This doesn't require the kind of cartridges used by long range shooters; instead, the .22 WRF Magnum, .22 Hornet, .218 Bee and .25-20 Winchester all are very practical choices and fun to shoot offhand. Prairie dogs, like woodchucks, are hunted with everything from .22 Long Rifle cartridges to those used for the world's biggest game, but the majority of hunters favor the centerfire .22 and 6mm calibers.

Handgunners find prairie dog villages excellent places to conduct what is called the "point-and-shoot" system. This is basically instinct shooting where the gunner carries the weapon casually and fires the instant a prairie dog head pops up without taking time to aim. Practice is needed to hone this skill to a fine edge, and dog towns supply the handgunner with plenty of opportunity.

Youngsters living in prairie dog country usually get their first shooting opportunity plinking away at these animals. Once they have been indoctrinated into firearms use and safety rules, prairie dogs are excellent targets for their initial trips afield. They guarantee plenty of action, and also provide practical experience in judging range and learning the basics of bullet performance.

Eastern varmint hunters who want a chance to make a prairie dog expedition now have plenty of assistance available, because there are at least four states in which there are outfitters who specialize in these animals. Most have, or can arrange, accommodations, meals, licenses

This light field-model bench by Tonoloway Tack Drivers, Inc., is perfect for setting up near prairie dog towns.

The portable Accuright Roto bench provides solid support for either handguns or rifles, and it's very portable.

and guides. The best reference to these services is *The Varmint Hunter*, the official publication of The Varmint Hunters Association, Inc.

Some outfitters include animals other than prairie dogs (some in the game category) in the package, so such ventures can be truly classed as "American safaris," on which several species can be collected in a single trip. They're also a lot less costly!

EQUIPMENT AND ACCESSORIES

Rifles have been discussed, but it's important to mention optics. The ranges involved and the conditions that exist make quality optics a

necessity. Variable rifle scopes and spotting scopes are the best, since they can be manipulated to help reduce mirage. Also, a good rangefinder will be very useful in estimating distance—an extremely difficult feat in flat country with so small an animal as a target.

Since prairie dogs are ordinarily shot from fixed positions and at long ranges, a steady shooting platform is essential. There are some very well-designed benches that fold down compactly and take up little room in a vehicle but can be erected in minutes. One- and two-man benches are available.

Good rests are essential. Shooting bags filled with sand or shot are probably the most commonly used, but there are several mechanical rifle rests available, some of which have adjustments for fine tuning the rifle's position. Bipods are useful on and off the bench, and there are models for both rifles and handguns. Shooters' tripods are also available.

Since intense heat, bright sunlight and wind are to be expected in prairie dog country, hunters should take along light, loose clothing, preferably long-sleeved shirts, and a broad-brimmed hat; sun screen; good shooting glasses; lip balm; and plenty of liquids.

7

Coyotes

The coyote belongs to the same family as the domestic dog, but except for some similarities in appearance with certain species such as the German shepherd, the resemblance ends there. To many, this animal is better characterized as one of man's worst enemies, and it is unquestionably one of the most persistent. Indian legend has it that the coyote will be the last animal remaining on earth before the world ends, and there is ample evidence to support this belief. No animal in North America possesses greater survival skills, and it's doubtful that any others can match wits with coyote. The Navaho Indians refer to the coyote as "God's dog" and rank its intelligence well above that of the wolf. Despite the popular myth that depicts the fox as the most cunning of all wild animals, an expert in predator control told me that "the dumbest coyote with half its brains knocked out has more sense than the smartest fox."

Other members of the Canidae clan are the wolves and foxes, but the coyote, *Canis latrans*, has proved to be the most adaptable and versatile of them all. According to location the color of the coat may vary considerably, but in gen-eral the upperparts are a grizzled gray, sometimes interspersed with brown or reddish tints, with buff undersides. The legs, feet and ears are yellowish to rusty, and the tail is bushy with a black tip. When running, the tail droops. Its general appearance is doglike, with prominent ears and a long, narrow muzzle. The coyote is extremely fast and agile and can move at speeds up to 40 mph, fast enough to roll a jack rabbit, but it usually cruises along at 25 to 30 mph. Weights are generally in the 20- to 50-pound range. It can also make leaps of up to 14 feet.

Coyotes communicate with a variety of vocal sounds—barks, yelps, howls and yaps—which are ordinarily heard at dusk, dawn or in the night. The calls help to keep members of the pack aware of each other's whereabouts and to reunite them when they become separated. Often one call will initiate a chorus of howling responses, resulting in the kind of eerie serenade that was frequently heard in old western movies while cowboys were gathered around a campfire. Barking alone usually signals a defensive attitude at the den or guarding a kill. Although coyotes hunt at night, they are equally active

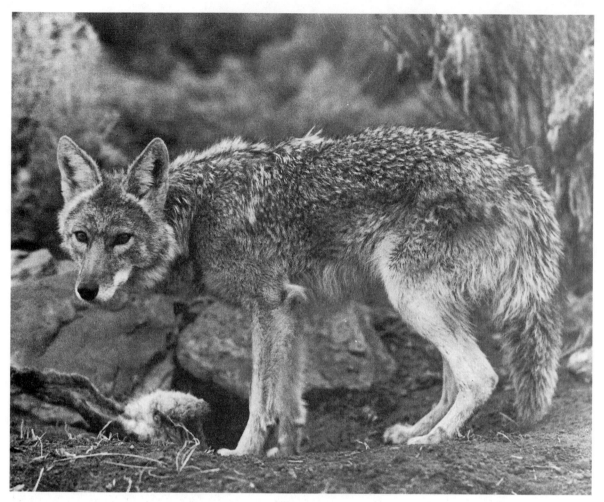

Coyote

during daylight hours, particularly when hunting rodents and other creatures that aren't moving about in darkness.

There is no particular habitat that can be described as typical, since these animals can adapt to almost any environment. In the West, coyotes are most commonly associated with open plains, while in the East, they prefer brushy areas. As population levels increase and more coyotes are in close proximity to populated areas, they are at home wherever they may be.

Coyotes mate for life, or at least for long periods, and travel as a pair during most of the year. They do not normally live in dens, but they select one as a nursery site before the pups are born. Dens may be in abandoned badger, fox or woodchucks burrows, in caves, hollow logs or culverts. The female may dig into the soft earth of river banks to create her own birthing chamber. Breeding takes place during February and April, with litters averaging six pups born in April and June of the following year. During this period, and until the pups are weaned and out on their own, the male and female are constant companions, with the male sharing the duties of parenthood. This is the time when adult animals are the most vulnerable, since much more food must be gathered to feed the young. This increases activity and causes coyotes to be more bold and aggressive.

Once the young are weaned and mobile, usually by late summer, parents abandon the den and the family travels together while the adults teach the pups how to obtain food. Small rodents, young birds, farm crops and road kills are typical beginners' fare. By late fall the young are on their own, living solitary lives and establishing their own territories.

The phenomenon of *coy-dog*, crosses between coyotes and domestic dogs, is much discussed among laymen, but this happens rarely and ordinarily only under certain circumstances.

Instances of this hybridization usually occur when coyotes move into a new area in which there often aren't enough of their own kind around. When the mating urge becomes strong in January and February and another coyote can't be found, a dog may be selected as a substitute. That's the only reason it happens, because coyotes prefer to breed with their own kind. Once enough coyotes are present, the dog reverts to the position of being just another part of their diet.

Coyote/wolf crosses have been documented, but coyote/fox interbreeding doesn't occur. Coyotes hate foxes and will kill adults and raid

Coyotes are widely distributed across the country. This one was photographed in the snows of Alaska.

dens to destroy and eat young pups. When coyote density increases in an area also inhabited by foxes, the population of the latter species invariably declines. It's a result of the well-known "peck order" in which the bigger and stronger species has the upper hand—or paw. This same situation occurs in places where wolf and coyote populations overlap, in which case the coyote is the loser.

Coyotes stake out individual territories with urine or feces, but they are always loosely associated and communicating with others in the vicinity. These come together as packs which at times travel and hunt together, allowing them to take on larger prey than a single animal could handle. This is a habit shared with their cousins, the wolves, and both species have some very sophisticated strategies much like military operations that involve luring, ambushing and swarming maneuvers.

Where food is concerned, there is almost no limit to what the omnivorous coyote can and will ingest. Rabbits, mice, gophers, ground squirrels, rats and voles are staple items. Included also are badgers, bobcats, peccaries, woodchucks, marmots, skunks, weasels, pheasants, quail and ducks. On up the scale, they readily take the young of deer, elk and antelope, and also the adult animals when they can bring them down. On the domestic side, they are serious predators of sheep, pigs, poultry and cattle. They also eagerly devour dogs and house cats.

That's not all. They are fond of all kinds of fruits and berries, grasshoppers and other insects, birds, frogs, salamanders, snakes, toads, corn, watermelons and cantaloupe. When times are tough they will eat carrion and cattle dung. Worst of all, they have been known to kill small children and attack adults.

The coyote's diet in the West isn't as diversified as in the East, where broader food choices can be found. A study conducted in Tennessee for several years by Memphis State University provides an idea of what they ingest in their southeastern range: 42.4 percent of the coyote stomachs contained rodent remains; 27.9 percent rabbit; 24.3 percent deer; 20.2 percent livestock; 13.5 percent insects; 11.9 percent nongame birds; 2.2 percent reptiles and amphibians; 1.1 percent shrews; 0.4 percent opossum; 31.5 percent persimmon; 21 percent other vegetation; 16 percent grass; 8 percent miscellaneous.

Except for man, the coyote is practically free from natural enemies throughout most of its range now that the bear and mountain lion numbers have diminished. However, these creatures never posed more than a token threat, even when their populations were high.

HISTORY

The history of the coyote in North America is one of constant range expansion. These animals were first documented in the United States more than 200 years ago along the Arizona-Mexican border. From this base, the animals began spreading northward through the western states, into Canada and Alaska. Next, they moved eastward through the Canadian provinces, the Midwest and on to the Northeast. The Southeast was the last region to be invaded, with the first animals appearing in the 1970s. Apparently the Mississippi River was for a long time a barrier to their usual west-to-east migrations. Today the coyote's range extends from Central America to Alaska and east to the Atlantic Ocean. Its common name was derived from the Nahuatl Indian word, *coyotl*, which means "barking dog." In the Southwest, *coyote* is usually pronounced *ki-o'-tee*, but in the northern and eastern part of its range, *ki'-oat* is more common. Cowboys often referred to them as "prairie warblers" or "ki-dogs."

The magnitude of this predator's impact wasn't realized until ranchers arrived in the Southwest, but the revelation wasn't long in coming. Calves and ewes were killed by the thousands, and maintaining herd populations in the face of the onslaught was often difficult. It was at this point that the coyote became the number one enemy of ranchers, and a war of eventually enormous proportions was initiated against them with its goal to eradicate the species.

It was a no-holds-barred effort in which every means conceivable was utilized. Shooting couldn't make a sufficient dent in their numbers, so traps, explosives, gas, poison and snares were added to the tools of combat. Later, aerial hunting was added. Bounties were offered, and the government also joined forces with the ranchers. How many animals were killed during the early years isn't known, but through the efforts of the Department of Agriculture's Animal Damage Control Program more than three and one-half million coyotes were eliminated between 1937 and 1981. This doesn't count animals destroyed by other agencies and individuals. Today, the cooperative predator control program destroys 65,000 to 85,000 coyotes annually at a cost of $11 million in funds made available by various state, federal, county and private sources.

As in the past, the eradication programs are carried out most aggressively in the western states, since this is where the greatest economic impact occurs. The problem is that advanced techniques haven't helped much, and Compound 1080, the most effective poison ever developed for use against the coyotes, continues to be banned by the federal government. Stockmen rail against the prohibition, because they claim that this is the only weapon that can save them from economic ruin, while opponents maintain that even Compound 1080 won't stop the coyote depredation and could endanger other species of wildlife.

All told, the effects of the reduction projects have been quite the opposite of what was intended. Instead of diminishing the species, coyotes have become even more numerous despite these efforts, and their range has continued to expand. Though once primarily associated with wild places, coyotes now frequent populated areas, foraging in city neighborhoods, robbing garbage cans and eating whatever else they can find, including domestic pets. In Los Angeles, which has one of the largest coyote populations of any major city, one study showed that 80 percent of their diet was dogs and cats.

What has maintained and increased coyote numbers is their amazing reproductive capabilities. Under pressure, litter sizes increase, and when it is removed fewer pups are born. Biologists call this a "density dependent" reproductive mechanism, similar to that which operates in rabbits. Evidence from studies shows that in Yellowstone National Park (where coyotes are protected) litters average one to two, but in places where they are heavily hunted and pursued the litter may be sixteen or more. An added element is that when these conditions exist, the animals are not only more fertile but also breed at younger ages.

The coyote problems in the West have been vexing enough, but the animal has become even more controversial in some of the other regions it occupies. In addition to continuing its assault on domestic livestock and farm crops, it is having a decided impact on antelope, deer and turkey populations. There is evidence that in some areas coyotes are killing up to twice as many deer as hunters, and there is also ample proof that the turkey population is being significantly reduced by this predator.

What happened in Nebraska is a good example of this problem. As more coyotes appeared in the state, the pronghorn antelope population began to dwindle. It was obvious that coyote predation was the reason. In a two-year study to reduce fawn mortality, game managers learned interesting facts about control measures. In the first year, 1990, they removed 112 coyotes from a 170-square-mile study area. Survival rates of pronghorn fawns rose to 62 percent inside the zone compared with 25 percent outside. The following year, they removed 88 coyotes from another 150-square-mile study area in which fawn survival jumped to 58 percent against the outside figure of 35 percent.

The conclusion was obvious: reduce coyote numbers and increased fawn survival rates will help assure stable antelope populations.

Another excellent illustration of this approach is seen in a Texas study involving coyote predation on whitetail deer fawns. The test site was a large ranch divided into two parts. On one half, coyote control measures were carried out, while coyotes occupying the other half were unmolested. The expected occurred: fawn survival rates rose by 500 percent in the section where coyotes were controlled as compared with the other half.

There are many other examples. Biologists in Minnesota believe that whitetail deer fawns comprise up to 70 percent of the coyote's diet in the months when birthing occurs, May through July, and much the same conclusion has been drawn in most other states where studies have been conducted. In Maine, New Hampshire, Vermont, New York and Massachusetts, deer populations are being heavily impacted. A Maine wildlife biologist, Henry Hilton, says that coyotes kill more than twice as many deer annually as do hunters.

Regardless of location, predation isn't limited to fawns. Coyotes kill thousands of adult deer, taking not just the old or weak animals but healthy ones, as well. Yearlings are particularly vulnerable to either individual animals or packs. This has a significant effect on wildlife management programs, even when deer populations are in good shape, since predation influences the buck/doe ratios biologists seek to establish in order to produce quality animals and maintain a good gene pool. For instance, if half of the fawns destroyed by coyotes are males, it's impossible to achieve the desired results.

So, looking at all of the problems the coyote poses for hunters, farmers and game biologists,

what are the prospects for finding some kind of solution? According to Gary Cook, a biologist with the Tennessee Wildlife Resources Agency and one of the top coyote experts in the East, they're good if the situation is viewed realistically.

"What's most important in any talk about coyotes is to recognize that this is a survivor that can adapt to any conditions. It's here to stay, and we have to look at how we can coexist with it and not make the same mistakes that have been made in the past by attempting to eradicate it with trapping, poisoning and bounty hunting. We've used everything short of atomic bombs as control measures, and none has succeeded. Proof of this is that there are more coyotes on the North American continent today than at any other time in history. The plain truth is that the coyote cannot be eliminated, and it will defeat any efforts we instigate to do so. If we're not intelligent enough by this time to understand this, we'd better give up and start over!

"Probably the best thing that can happen is for hunters to recognize that the coyote is the most intelligent and challenging animal they're ever likely to seek. As such, coyotes are truly trophy animals, as worthy of bragging about as an eight-point buck. It takes a particular type of hunter to get good at killing coyotes, too. You have to work at it, because if you don't the animal will make a fool of you early in the game.

"What we and other agencies across the country have done is to enlist the aid of hunters, explaining that by learning coyote control techniques they can form mutually beneficial associations with landowners. Coyote control has become a necessary part of farm maintenance, and if a hunter can get good at harvesting them, he can open up land for other kinds of hunting. In the old days, when farmers had predator problems, they called in the hunters, so the coyote offers a chance to revive that tradition.

"These ideas are catching on, and more varmint hunters are finding that hunting coyotes is more exciting and enjoyable than some other forms of the sport, and also more varied."

Many different kinds of coyote control measures have been devised for landowners. Electric fences are especially useful for tracts of up to about a hundred acres, but unlike the common one- or two-strand types, these have seven strands that don't permit getting under or over the charge. Game agencies also supply landowners with information and instructions on how to trap coyotes. This requires special techniques, since coyotes are extremely cautious and instinctively wary of devices intended to end their lives. They learn to spot trap sets. There have been occasions when coyotes have picked up traps and deposited them elsewhere without setting them off.

"Guard dogs are helpful," says Cook, "especially big animals such as the Pyrenees, a gentle species, but with enough bulk to be intimidating to coyotes who see them in the fields or on farm premises."

Cook says that total elimination of coyotes is a bad idea because:

"First of all, it isn't possible, and second, there's a place for these animals in the overall picture. Coyotes eliminate a great many rodents, and not all are guilty of causing farmers grief.

"The way to view this is to look for the few coyotes in an area that are causing damage. For example, a farmer may have a large tract of land frequented by as many as a hundred coyotes and still have no problems, while the farm next door may have one coyote which has developed a taste for poultry, livestock or maybe the watermelon patch. That's the animal that should be eliminated instead of declaring war on all coyotes in the area. As with people, a couple of bad actors can give a neighborhood a bad name."

Strangely, there are people who like to eulogize carnivores such as grizzly bears, mountain lions, wolves and coyotes, claiming that they are noble creatures and symbols of nature. They view them as underdogs—man being the ruthless villain threatening their existence.

It is a false premise, particularly in the case of the coyote, since human existence is ultimately more threatened than that of this daring and durable animal. Something else: hunters and trappers recognize and respect the coyote's intelligence and ability to survive.

The truth is that the coyote is a cold-blooded killer that relentlessly stalks calves, ewes and fawns. Anyone who sees a coyote eagerly gobble down a newborn fawn and walk away, will surely conclude that it is a cunning, vicious marauder.

HUNTING METHODS

Coyotes have been hunted on foot and on horseback, in vehicles, and in airplanes and helicopters. In recent years, these mechanized methods have become illegal in most places, with only government predator-control personnel allowed to use them.

Calling

Predator calling totally revolutionized coyote hunting, and it stands as the most important tactic a hunter can employ in killing not only coyotes but also a number of other pest animals.

It isn't a recent development. The late J. Murray Burnham, a Texan, is acknowledged as the father of predator calling. Burnham stumbled upon the idea early in the century when he was a young boy. He observed a jack rabbit tangled in a barbed wire fence, emitting screams of pain. Moments later, three wolves came running in and quickly devoured it. Realizing that the animal's distress calls were what attracted the wolves, Burnham began practicing making the sounds with his mouth, and within a short time had the mimicry perfected.

To test out his new skill, he took a companion along and returned to the same spot where the jack rabbit had met its end. They both had rifles. The unexpected happened. Just as they arrived at the scene, they saw seven wolves in pursuit of a doe, which they quickly brought

Predator calls were invented by J. Murray Burnham in the 1920s, and since that time a great many variations have been produced. This is an assortment of mouth calls.

down and began to tear apart. Burnham pulled his companion down behind a log and began calling. The effect was far beyond what he had expected. An old wolf standing guard while the others ate immediately came running straight to the call, and seconds later the others abandoned the dead doe and followed. Both boys started shooting, and by the time the wolves finally dispersed and ran, four of them lay dead.

From that point Burnham's reputation as a predator killer grew. At one time, responding to a plea from a rancher whose land was overrun with foxes, he called in and killed 105 in six hours. He kept reducing them throughout the year and ended with a total of 451.

Burnham developed the manual, or mouth call, which remains as deadly today as when he first used it. It's a simple process but one that requires some practice and experimentation. Here's how it's done:

Begin by getting the inside of your mouth as dry as possible by swallowing several times. Then open your mouth slightly and pull your lips over your teeth, at the same time gently sucking in air, using your mouth as a sort of reverse bellows. Keep at it, varying the pressure on your lips until you begin producing some squeaking sounds. Once this is accomplished, keep practicing until you can get consistent tones. After that, the sounds can be manipulated by cupping one of your hands over your mouth and moving it back and forth or bringing it closer to mute the call when an animal is extremely close. Eventually, the process feels

A closer view of some predator calls, including the popular bulb-type mouse squeaker at extreme left.

This Knight & Hale predator kit comes with three calls and an instructional tape.

natural, and creating the sounds is almost effortless.

Although this technique is still useful, there are now several manufactured calls that reproduce the rabbit distress cries and many other sounds that attract predators. J. Murray Burnham himself invented a number of these, as well as calls designed to lure other animals. His two sons, Murray and Winston, carried on the tradition, forming Burnham Brothers Company and eventually expanding the selection beyond mouth and hand-operated calls to electronic devices that offer a wide variety of sounds. These have significant advantages, the principal one being that the sounds are generated from tapes or computer chips and are duplications of the actual distress sounds made by various creatures. Among these are rabbit shrieks; mouse squeaks; coyote and fox pup yowls; woodpecker screeches; fawn, calf and ewe bawls; and other signals that something is dying and it's time for the coyote to move in and get its share. These units are light, compact and easily portable. Another prominent predator call company, Johnny Stewart, even produces a battery-operated device that can be worn on the belt and plays miniature records.

Even with the authenticity of the sounds produced by electronic calls, hunters who use them almost always also employ conventional calls to obtain maximum results. This permits additional sounds to be mixed in, and both the volume and the tempo of the mouth-operated models can be adjusted according to how the coyote is reacting.

For beginning varmint hunters, the electronic

Electronic calls have come a long way in recent years. This Burnham Brothers electronic model is computerized and very compact. All of the items fit into a small handbag.

Another popular electronic call is the Johnny Stewart model, which comes with a variety of tapes for hunting many kinds of predators.

A coyote hunter inserts a tape into a Johnny Stewart electronic call.

This short-range, battery-operated electronic call can be worn on the belt.

calls provide a special benefit. Listening to the actual bird and animal sounds and trying to duplicate them as closely as possible works a lot better than trying to learn by reading instruction books.

Being successful on a regular basis requires more than just calling. The craftiness and intelligence of the animal has already been described, but something else is worth adding: the coyote possesses eyesight and hearing as keen as that of

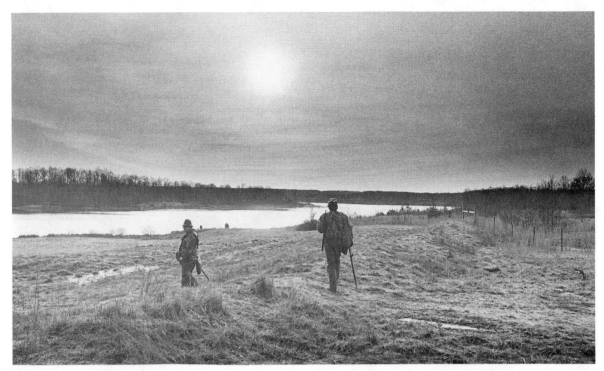

A pair of coyote hunters moving into position in a frost-covered field in early morning.

the wild turkey, along with an equal amount of wariness. What makes it even more elusive and hard to fool is that it also can *smell.*

When hunting in daylight, wear full camouflage and remain as motionless as possible. As with turkey hunting, it's best to have your gun in a position for a quick shot and with a minimum of motion.

There's a difference in hunting open country and in woods or broken country where visibility is limited. In open country, you can often see approaching coyotes at a distance, giving you time to prepare. Just as important, you can gauge its reactions to your call. In tighter cover the coyote may be almost upon you before you see it.

There are several factors that influence how a coyote responds to a call. If the animal is very hungry, it's likely to exhibit less caution. Young coyotes who haven't had contact with such situations also tend to be easier to lure in. The placement of the caller is important, too. Some

This big male coyote was called in and killed in the woods as it foraged for rodents.

A hunter calls a coyote in open country in South Dakota.

kinds of locations suggest a trap, and the animals will avoid them. Coyotes almost invariably approach prey from downwind, and when in more dense cover, it's necessary to get off a shot before the coyote picks up the human scent.

Hunters in open country often use rifles to pick off the animals at long range. Of the favorite coyote cartridges, the .243 Winchester, .25-06 Remington and 6mm Remington stand out as the top three. All have sufficient punch to cleanly kill a coyote, whereas the .222 and .223 Remington are a little light and sometimes don't perform as effectively. Many hunters use larger calibers—.270 Winchester, .30-06 Springfield, 7mm Remington Magnum and even some of the big boomers like the 300 Weatherby Magnum or .375 H&H Magnum—since coyotes are excellent target practice for big game.

In places where night hunting is allowed, the shotgun is often the weapon of choice, because all shots can be made at very close range. Again, it's important to select the proper gauge and shot size. Nobody can argue with a 12 gauge and loads of 00 buckshot as an adequate exterminator, but pattern the gun in advance to see how broadly the shot are distributed at the approximate 40-yard range at which most coyotes are killed. The goal is to get as many of the big pellets into the animal as possible.

Daytime hunting in heavy cover is also a good place for a shotgun, although some hunters prefer rifles with open sights.

Scouting an area before setting up to call and hunt is always wise. If there are coyotes in the vicinity, finding sign isn't difficult. Coyotes move around a lot; their preferred paths are along trails, dirt roads or around the perimeters of open fields or waterholes. There will be an abundance of droppings along such routes, and plenty of tracks. These are the best places to set up. Choose a place where you have a good field of view, away from bushes or timber. Coyotes determined to investigate a call will cross open country without hesitation. If it's necessary to set up in the woods, you're likely to have only brief glimpses, if any, of the predator.

Probably the most valuable thing a hunter can do to learn about coyotes or other predators is to call them in and observe their behavior without shooting. You'll acquire a storehouse of information that will prove extremely valuable and will inevitably improve your hunting skills. The hunter-predator game is always won by the smartest of the adversaries, so a hunter never can know too much about any critter.

This kind of practice calling can have drawbacks, though. If the animal spots you or is in some way alarmed, it may become call shy and be difficult or impossible to lure in again. This is especially true when calling young animals during late summer and early fall, because these are the ones you'll be hunting in the winter and spring. The best solution is to use a different sound when practice calling than the one you employ when actually hunting.

Something to remember is that coyotes will respond to calls as readily during the day as at night, so if hunting after dark isn't allowed where you live, it isn't a disadvantage. Night hunting simply embodies a few more thrills and excitement because there's so little visibility and things can happen so quickly.

Decoys

One of the most deadly tactics is the use of decoys.

There are a number of decoys that can be used, some of which are applicable year-round, and others that have great appeal only seasonally. During the months when does are giving birth, newborn fawns are a favorite coyote food. At this time, an antelope or deer fawn decoy can provoke a hungry coyote to lose all caution and come racing in for an easy meal.

Fawn decoys can be easily made by obtaining a form from a taxidermist and using spray paint to create the right color pattern. It doesn't have to be exact: even a general resemblance to a fawn is enough to bring in a coyote. Hunters using this method rack up high scores for as long as the birthing season lasts. After that, fawn decoys have some value, but there are other kinds that are better.

One of these is a rabbit decoy, which can be either a mounted specimen or one of the stuffed animals that can be bought in a toy store. The advantage of the manufactured kind is that some are battery-equipped and display movement, usually in the ears. This is a critical advantage,

When deer are giving birth, a fawn decoy is extremely effective in luring coyotes. Later, rabbit decoys are better.

because coyotes have extremely good vision, and they can spot movement from far away.

Other stuffed animal toys also work. Dogs are probably the second choice of most hunters (and again, if they exhibit motion, all the better). Possibly cats and teddy bears would work, too. The main thing is to have an object that catches the attention of the coyote while the caller, or callers, work the animal into a feeding frenzy.

Long-Range Hunting

This is a sport that attracts a large number of participants. Most long-range hunting is done on the Great Plains, where there are plenty of wide-open spaces, but there are many places in the East where similar types of terrain can be found.

These shooters set up on a small rise or hill where they can observe a lot of territory. They glass the area until they spot a coyote. It may be that the animal is 300 yards away, or maybe 600 yards, but that's where the challenge lies. This breed of rifle hunters yearn for ultra-long-range opportunities, and their rifles reflect this urge. The .220 Swift and .22-250 Remington are favorites for super-long shots. Coyotes passing closer may be taken with a .25-06 Remington or .243 Winchester. Because they usually drive right up to the spot where they intend to set up, hunters can carry all the gear and rifles they want.

For these hunters, the action may be somewhat slower than for callers, but since their main goal is accurate bullet placement, how many coyotes they bag isn't all that important.

Bowhunting

Bowhunters are getting into coyote hunting in increasing numbers. With calls the animals can be brought within shooting range. Since the bow is relatively silent, a miss may not alarm a coyote, unless it has spotted your movement, giving you time for a second shot. The twin challenges of calling and using primitive equipment are especially satisfying to bow hunters.

In the Northeast, where packs of hounds are used to pursue bears and bobcats, hunters have discovered that coyotes provide plenty of sport off-season. This isn't a new idea. Many years ago some southern fox hunters imported a few coyotes to see if they would provide the same amount of sport as their cousins, but the experiment didn't prove successful. The remnants of this unauthorized stocking became the first coyotes to inhabit the Southeast before the major invasion.

One other kind of hunter deserves to be mentioned, even though this person doesn't contribute to the reduction of coyote numbers. This is the individual who hunts with a camera, using the same tactics and techniques. The coyote's sensitive ears almost always pick up the click of the shutter, and this makes every photo opportunity a one-shot proposition. Actually, there are quite a few gun hunters who carry a camera and switch off occasionally to press a shutter release instead of squeezing a trigger. It's a satisfying alternative.

EQUIPMENT AND ACCESSORIES

It's been explained that *total* camouflage is very important when hunting coyotes, so those who plan to hunt these animals throughout the year will require a variety of patterns to match seasonal conditions, and they will also need clothing for different weather conditions. For concealing the face, some hunters like nets while others prefer camouflage grease paint, which can't catch on twigs or branches.

Often there's adequate natural cover available, but if not, there are a number of excellent light, portable blinds on the market that are easy to set up and work very well. Some are even reasonably weatherproof.

The right kind of masking scent is very useful in preventing a coyote approaching downwind from detecting your presence. Skunk odor is particularly effective for this purpose.

It's important to have a number of different

Where night hunting is permitted, lights like these will handle all of a hunter's needs. The top four are Coleman hand-held lights, the most powerful of which is the one-million candlepower unit on the left. Below, left to right, are the TopSpot, which can be worn as a head light or folded up and hand held; the Browning Lightning Bug head light; and the Browning Micro Ballistic Lite.

calls. Situations differ and sometimes a particular sound is required. Calls shouldn't be selected at random, but rather added once their value in the field has been established. Advice from experienced hunters will help in picking the right ones.

If you plan to hunt at night, there are numerous kinds of lights developed specifically for varmint hunters, including hand-held spotlights and ones that plug into automobile cigarette lighter sockets and generate up to one million candlepower. Headlights are very handy, as are the lights that attach to a gun barrel. A red lens prevents spooking the animals. The theory is that this reduces the heat produced by white light, which the eyes of predators can't tolerate. It isn't the illumination that matters, but the *kind* of illumination.

8

Foxes

The sly, clever fox is well known to the American public, for it has long been the subject of songs, children's stories, comic books and animated cartoons, usually acting the villain. In addition, the word *fox* is commonly used in various ways, some derogatory, some complimentary.

What brought about the fox's "bad guy" reputation is its fondness for domestic fowl, particularly chickens. Foxes are notorious for their midnight raids on hen houses, and they won't pass up the chance to grab a duck, goose or turkey. The economic impact is small, but the level of indignation is high.

Hunters view the fox quite differently, because its cunning and intelligence pose a formidable challenge few other animals can match. Trying to "outfox the fox" is always a tough proposition, regardless of what hunting method is employed. No one who has pursued this cunning canine can help but respect its ability to outsmart both men and dogs.

There are four major species of foxes on the North American continent, and their distribution is such that almost no place is without one or more of them. The ones best known are the

Red Fox and Gray Fox, since their ranges are the most extensive. The others are the Swift or Kit Fox and the Arctic Fox. All are members of the Canidae family, which also includes the wolves and the coyote.

RED FOX

The most abundant species of them all, the red fox is indigenous to America, although some of the early settlers were apparently unaware of the fact. In the mid-eighteenth century, wealthy landowners in New York, Maryland, New Jersey, Delaware and Virginia who enjoyed the English tradition of riding to the hounds were stymied by the gray fox's ability to climb trees. To bring the sport up to par, they imported red foxes from England, only to discover later that there were already native red foxes in the region.

As a result, the native and imported stock intermingled and the range kept expanding until virtually all of the continent was populated. Much of the growth came about as a result of land being cleared for farms. This activity provided ideal habitat for the red fox,

Red Fox

which likes open areas bounded by woodlands and brushy fencerows that offer protection. The coming of agriculture also brought about a great increase in rabbits and other small rodents which comprise a large part of the fox's diet.

With the increase in population, additional pressure was put on the red fox. Its fur became highly popular for women's coats and neck pieces, and it was subjected to extensive trapping. Since foxes preyed on domestic fowl, farmers demanded their elimination, so bounties were placed on them in many places. Both forces took a heavy toll on the animals, but as trapping became regulated and commercial fox farms began producing more pelts, fewer wild animals were captured. The bounty system proved unsatisfactory, and eventually all states ceased the practice. And finally, farmers learned how to foxproof their chicken pens, so that form of opposition all but vanished.

The red fox is the largest of the species, attaining weights of up to 15 pounds. Most often, it displays the color for which it was named, a golden-red. This dominates the upperparts from its black nose to the end of its bushy, white-tipped tail. The belly, chin and throat are white, and the feet, backs of the ears and sometimes parts of the tail are black. There are silver, black, brown and intermediate color phases, but all have the white-tipped tail.

Red foxes sometimes attain weights of up to 15 pounds, but their bushy fur makes them appear to be larger.

Red foxes are omnivorous and ingest a wide variety of foods. During the summer months they eat berries, grapes, cherries, apples, peaches, cantaloupe, corn, grasses, acorns and a variety of invertebrates that includes beetles, grasshoppers, crickets, caterpillars, salamanders and crayfish. They prey on rabbits, woodchucks, squirrels, quail, pheasants and various other kinds of birds and rodents year-round, but these are the main food sources during the winter months.

Dens are used only for maternity purposes. These may be located in caves, hollow trees or logs, rock and brush piles, or in excavations they make on hillsides or along stream banks.

Mounds of dirt covering food caches are usually close by. Mating takes place in January and February, with litters of one to ten born fifty-one to fifty-three days later. The kits begin to emerge from the dens at about one month of age and disperse at four months, and the den is abandoned.

In the winter red foxes usually sleep in the open, curled up into a ball with the bushy tail acting as a blanket. They remain comfortable even when covered by snow, and often they burrow into it for added warmth and protection. Much of their foraging is done at night, but in lean times they move about as readily in

Red fox kits emerge from the den at one month of age. At four months they disperse, and the den is abandoned.

daylight hours. Owing to their shy, wary nature, they are seldom seen even by people living near their habitat.

Their range covers all of Canada except small parts of British Columbia and Saskatchewan, and all but the extreme northern parts of Alaska. They're found everywhere except in southwestern California, Utah, Nevada, Arizona, northwest Texas and the coastal region from North Carolina to Florida.

Experts put the red fox population at three to four million and predict continued expansion unless competition with the coyote blocks or slows its growth.

GRAY FOX

Although the showy red fox is the species most familiar to the public, a the smaller gray fox easily matches it in grace and beauty. The upperparts are a grizzled gray, and the underparts and back of the head reddish. The throat is white, and the feet rusty colored. The tail is black on top, with a black tip. It weighs between 7 and 13 pounds.

The gray fox can climb trees, allowing it to harvest fruits and nuts before they fall and can be eaten by ground-bound animals. Grays often take refuge in trees when pursued, or use them as resting places.

Like the red fox, it is omnivorous, with a major part of its diet consisting of cottontail rabbits, rats, mice, voles and many other small mammals and birds. It eats various kinds of plant material, including grasses, persimmons, grapes, apples, cherries, blackberries, acorns, pokeweed fruit and strawberries. It also forages for insects, salamanders, small snakes and crayfish. The gray fox doesn't have the red fox's reputation for stealing chickens, but occasional cases of missing domestic fowl can be traced to them.

Dens are most often in natural openings such as rock crevices, caves, abandoned woodchuck burrows, hollow trees or logs, rock and brush piles or under boulders. They sometimes den under abandoned farm buildings. The dens are used all winter for shelter and safety, and most often the same sites are used year after year, either by the same animals or succeeding generations.

Mating takes place in February and March,

Gray Fox

with litters of two to seven pups born in March or April. The young are weaned in three months and are on their own at four months.

The range of the gray fox is almost entirely in the United States, with only a couple of small intrusions into Canada. It is found in all of the eastern states west to North and South Dakota, Nebraska, Kansas and Oklahoma; also in most of Texas, New Mexico, Arizona, California, eastern Oregon, the southern parts of Utah and Nevada, and Colorado. There is one species related to the gray fox, the insular gray fox, which occurs as six subspecies on six islands off the California coast.

OTHER FOXES

The **Arctic Fox** changes colors with the seasons, going from brown to white as winter begins as a means of matching the environment. An uncommon blue phase is a dark blue-gray in summer, and a pale blue-gray in winter.

This is an animal of the Far North, and typical of all creatures that inhabit deserts, hot or frigid, it has special physical attributes. The most obvious are its short legs and compact body that help to reduce heat loss, and the thick fur that helps to contain it. It also has hairy foot pads that provide both insulation and traction on icy surfaces.

Arctic foxes eat almost anything they can catch, find or steal. Lemmings are a main food source in the summer, along with young arctic or snowshoe hares, the eggs and young of birds, fish, berries and some plant material. In winter they depend heavily on carrion, and they follow polar bears in order to scavenge the leftovers from their kills. It isn't unusual for these animals to forage for distances as much as a thousand miles. At times when food is abundant, it is stored in holes dug into the permafrost.

The range of the arctic fox extends from northern and western Alaska into Canada south to the Northwest Territories, and into northern Alberta,

Manitoba and Quebec. Its principal enemy is the trapper, but with the decrease in fur sales, the population has risen sharply. This has caused more serious depredation on nesting waterfowl and other birds which nest within its range.

There are two other fox species that are sometimes linked together, but differences in ranges and physical characteristics make it clear that they are not the same.

The **Kit Fox** is a small, slender animal, yellowish in color, with large ears and a black-tipped tail. Its range is fairly broad, extending south from southeastern Oregon and including parts of California, Nevada, Utah, New Mexico and Texas. It is also found in western and central Mexico.

The kit fox eats small rodents, insects, berries, lizards and snakes. It is seldom sought by man, and its natural enemies are eagles and coyotes.

The **Swift Fox** is a creature of the high plains and prairies, and one of the fastest of all of the foxes. Tawny colored, with a black-tipped tail, it bears a close resemblance to the kit fox. Both weigh between 3 and 6 pounds, and as its name implies, the swift fox is very fast.

The range extends from southern Alberta, Saskatchewan and Manitoba southward, including the eastern half of Montana and Wyoming, eastern Colorado, northeastern New Mexico, northwestern Texas, all of North Dakota, South Dakota and Nebraska, the extreme western parts of Minnesota and Iowa, and western Kansas and Oklahoma.

Rabbits, mice, rats, squirrels and other small rodents are mainstay diet items, along with birds, snakes, lizards, berries, nuts and other vegetable matter.

Destruction of its habitat threatened the swift fox for a time, but it is now protected in some areas as an endangered species and is holding its own.

HUNTING METHODS

To most, the mention of foxes brings to mind people attired in red coats, white breeches and

All foxes have keen eyesight, and good camouflage is an asset in hunting them.

polished boots riding on horseback behind hounds hot on the trail of their quarry, or a group of overall-clad men sitting around a campfire telling tall tales and listening to the exciting bugling of the foxhounds coursing through the nearby woodlands. And maybe taking an occasional swing from a jug to ward off the real or imagined chill of the night.

Varmint hunters see foxes in a different way, since they have to compete with them on even terms. Even though the intelligence of foxes doesn't compare with coyotes, they're far from being slouches where wariness and cunning are concerned. Plenty of hunters have been thoroughly duped by foxes, and those who haven't are almost certain to have it in their future.

Trapping and following the hounds once accounted for the majority of foxes taken, but once predator calling came onto the scene, the situation changed dramatically. Varmint hunters have become proficient in the art of luring them in, and this has broadened the scope of the sport.

In the northern states where winter snow is dependable, certain conditions make it possible to trail foxes and overtake them. Red foxes carry their tails low, and when traveling in wet or melting snow, the tails accumulate a load of slush and ice, the weight of which eventually

exhausts the animal. Without strength to continue, the fox becomes easy prey for a hunter.

Hunting bedded foxes in the snow is another popular method, which requires finding tracks and following them to where the fox is nestled down in the snow. Because walking in the snow, and especially in crusty snow, is noisy, a very stealthy approach is necessary. A better tactic is to call, arouse the animal and coax it in.

Another stillhunting technique is to locate the trails foxes routinely use when foraging and wait for them to appear. Since foxes are primarily nocturnal, the early-morning and late-afternoon periods are when they are most likely to be seen.

Many of the same sounds used to attract coyotes and bobcats work well on both the gray and red species, although they have their own peculiarities and habits that makes hunting them a specific art. Also, different tactics are required for each because they don't usually occupy the same kinds of habitat. It's not possible to cover all of the details involved in the predator calling game in this volume, but there's a book that fully explains its mysteries: *Murray Burnham's Hunting Secrets.* This is the predator caller's bible and is an invaluable reference for both novice and experienced hunters.

If you're in a place where night hunting is

When night hunting, a good spotlight is necessary. This hand-held Coleman spotlight produces one-million candlepower.

permitted, this is by far the most productive period, and moonless nights are always the best. Foxes are nocturnal and on the prowl for food, which makes them especially susceptible to calls imitating the prey they seek. Since foxes don't try to bring down animals larger than themselves, the distress sounds of rabbits or mouse squeaks are the most effective.

In night calling for foxes and all other species, the light used to illuminate the hunting zone should remain on at all times, since turning it on and off can be distracting to both the hunter and the quarry. A red or orange light doesn't frighten foxes, regardless of how it's directed, but the beam of a white light should be kept above ground level. There are many ways to manipulate a beam, some of them relating to whether it's operated from a vehicle or from a

hunter's headlight. The best combination is a red light for seeing the animal's eyes, and a white light mounted on the gun barrel that can be turned on when it's time to shoot.

Scouting areas you plan to hunt is important in deciding where to set up after darkness. Fox sign is similar to that of coyotes, but because foxes are much smaller and lighter, their tracks are usually very difficult to discern. The scat usually contains hair, since rodents are a principal food source, but if this is absent, it can mean that they are feeding mostly on other things. Rodents mean open spaces, while other contents may suggest wooded or brushy locations, and it will assist in deciding where to position yourself. Foxes are much more inclined to use the same game routes of travel, which are usually game and livestock trails and country

This Nite Lite mounts on the barrel or scope and can be turned on at the last minute before squeezing the trigger to illuminate the target.

Killing foxes lured in with predator calls is best accomplished with a 12-gauge shotgun, since the body size of these animals is smaller than the profile suggests. From top, three good choices are the Winchester 1300 pump, Winchester 1400 automatic and Mossberg 3½-inch Magnum.

roads, and the amount of scat found at these locations is a measure of the number of foxes that are in the vicinity.

EQUIPMENT AND ACCESSORIES

Since foxes can be called in to close range, especially at night, a shotgun is the best choice. The animal's bushy fur makes it look a lot bigger than it really is, and the chances of missing it or not hitting a vital spot with a rifle in semi-darkness are very high. A full-choked 12-gauge shotgun loaded with high-brass or magnum shells and No. 2 or No. 4 shot sizes will do the job very well. If a rifle is preferred, the .17 Remington, .22 Hornet, .25-20 Winchester and .32-20 Winchester are good choices.

Foxes often respond to calls very quickly, so

electronic calls aren't recommended. Manual types are better, since the tones and volume can be matched to the situation and the animal's reactions.

At times, insects can be a problem at night, and repellants can be useful. However, be sure to select one with a scent that won't be a handicap.

The Winchester Model 70 in .22-250 with a Bausch & Lomb 6×-24× scope and a pair of Bausch & Lomb Elite binoculars are excellent equipment for shooting foxes at long range.

9

Bobcats

Of the seven members of the cat family found in North America, only one, the bobcat or wildcat, is given serious consideration by varmint hunters. The main reason for this may be their wide distribution and the great capacity they display in being able to adapt to changing environmental conditions.

This cat's common name comes from its short, stubby tail. With the exception of its cousin, the lynx, it is the only native feline with such an appendage. Normally, a feline's long tail is very important in maintaining balance when climbing and leaping, yet the bobcat seems to manage both quite well despite its absence.

Although there are some variations from one location to another, the basic color of the bobcat is pale to reddish-brown with indistinct black spots and streaks above, and a whitish color below. The tail is black above and white below, and the ears slightly tufted. Weights vary fairly widely, generally ranging between 14 and 40 pounds, but specimens of up to 69 pounds have been recorded. Males are larger than the females, from 28 to 49 inches long.

Part of the differences in sizes and weights reflect the type of country in which they're found, but genetic differences are also responsible in part for these variations. Throughout the United States there are nine subspecies, each of which exhibits some specific identifying characteristics.

The bobcat is a very efficient hunter, and meat is the primary item in its diet. Rabbits, squirrels, mice, rats, porcupines and a variety of other rodents, small mammals and birds are included, as well as domestic fowl. A big adult bobcat can bring down an antelope or a full-grown deer. Carrion is eaten only on rare occasions. With the rapidly increasing wild turkey populations across the country, both young and adult birds have become a favorite target of these cats. Some hunting is done from trees, where it perches and waits for prey to appear, but it operates mostly on the ground. Its mottled fur is an excellent camouflage.

Normally, if food availability is good and little hunting pressure is exerted, a bobcat's range can be as small as five miles in diameter, yet otherwise it may be as large as fifty miles.

Many of the calls bobcats make are sometimes mistaken for those of house cats, except

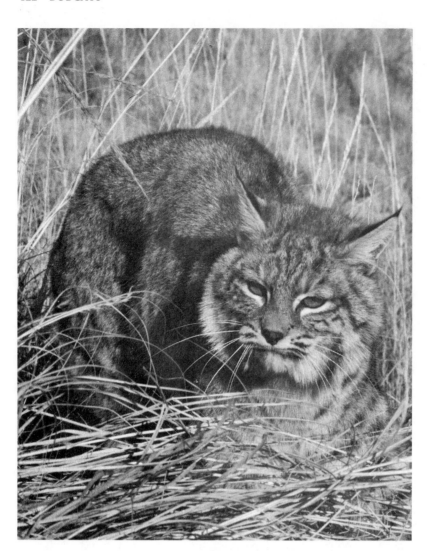

Bobcat

for their high, piercing scream, which has been likened to that of a terrified woman.

Bobcats use thickets, caves and brushpiles as hiding places during the day, conducting most of their hunting at night. At times when food is scarce, they also forage during daylight hours. They are good swimmers, but they usually enter the water only when pursued and no other alternative escape route exists. Areas with scrubby or second-growth forests and fairly rugged terrain are favored habitat, but they also adapt well to mountainous areas and swamps. Owing to their shyness and stealth, they can live close to populated areas without the residents ever being aware of their presence. At times they compete with raccoons and opossums for dog and cat food left on back porches or in yards.

Breeding takes place in the spring, with a litter of between two and four born in late April or early May. Once the female is close to giving birth, she drives the male away, because it is likely to devour the young. The helpless kittens are too tempting and easy a meal to pass up. Maternity dens are likely to be in hollow logs, dense brushpiles or rock shelters. The young begin hunting with their mother at about seven months, then become independent at about nine to twelve months.

There are records of crosses between bobcats and housecats, but this occurs rarely.

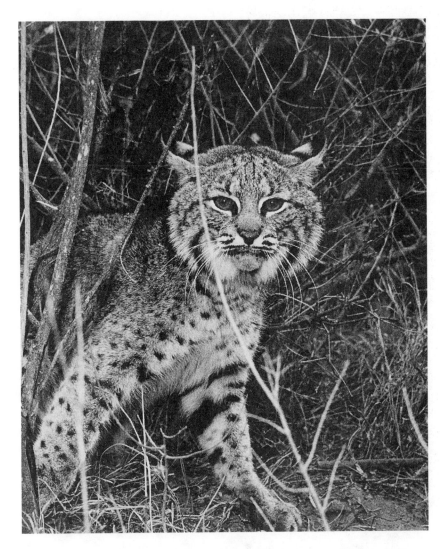

Bobcats usually hunt at night. During the day, they hide in thickets, caves and brush piles.

Adults lead solitary lives except during the mating season, and males and females have separate territories that seldom overlap. Like many animals, they urinate on rocks or trees to establish scent posts defining their sector of operations, and often the scat also serves this purpose. Bobcats are very fastidious about burying their fecal matter. There's an Indian legend that expresses the belief that such deposits eventually turn into precious jewels, which is why they're so well concealed. However, why this would be of concern to the bobcat is impossible to fathom.

The bobcat ranges from coast to coast across the United States and into Mexico and the extreme southern parts of all of the Canadian provinces. The highest populations exist in the western states, but since intensive trapping of the animals has diminished, they are making good comebacks in many of the eastern states. The only region where they are conspicuously absent is in the central to lower Midwest. Enemies of adult animals other than man are wolves, coyotes and domestic dogs. Kittens are sometimes preyed upon by foxes and horned owls. At one time there was a strong demand for bobcat fur, and trappers vigorously sought the animals. Today, with the prices down, there are much fewer taken in this manner.

Closely associated with the bobcat in appearance and habits is the **Lynx**, but its range and habits cause it to be of only minor interest to varmint hunters. However, it's a worthy adversary, because it possesses all of the stealth and elusiveness of its close cousin.

The range of the lynx includes all of Canada and Alaska except the extension of the Great Plains that lies in southern Alberta, Saskatchewan and Manitoba. In the United States it occupies only parts of Washington, northern Oregon and Idaho, a very small part of Montana, and a few Rocky Mountain locations in Wyoming and Colorado. Northern Wisconsin, Minnesota and Michigan have populations. In the East, a few are found in northern New England and New York.

Well-adapted to its northern range, the lynx is heavily furred, including its feet, which allows it to move silently and rapidly through the snow. Its color is a tawny buff, with brownish underparts. Its tail is short, but longer than the bobcat's, and it has tufted ears and pale cheek ruffs that form a beard at the throat. Males are larger than the females and may weigh up to 60 pounds.

Mostly nocturnal, the lynx stays hidden by day under fallen trees, low-hanging evergreen limbs or rock ledges. Like the bobcat, it is an expert climber and often hunts from trees. Snowshoe hares are its principal prey, although a variety of small rodents and mice are also mainstays. The remains of large game animals, moose, caribou, sheep and deer supply food in the winter months. It caches leftovers under snow for future meals. Livestock are sometimes targets of the lynx, but this usually occurs on farms in remote areas.

Man has long been a major enemy of the lynx, since its long, silky fur has been of prime market value. Wolves and mountain lions are its only other threat.

The tawny-colored **Mountain Lion**, also known as puma, cougar, panther and cata-

Mountain Lion

mount, is the largest of North American purring cats, weighing up to 275 pounds. While it is the most widely distributed, its numbers are far below those of the bobcat, but this has not always been the case. Once the mountain lion was found from coast to coast and from British Columbia to South America. A superior predator capable of killing large animals, wild and domestic, it became the number one enemy of cattle and sheep ranchers early on, and later of game officials in some places. As a result, their numbers and range have been reduced enormously. While still hunted in areas where they are abundant, they are fully protected in most states in which only small populations remain.

The major concentrations of mountain lions are presently found from British Columbia and southern Alberta south into Mexico, including parts of Washington, Oregon, California, Montana, Idaho, Wyoming, Utah, Colorado, Arizona, New Mexico and Texas. Limited populations occur in Louisiana, Tennessee, Alabama and Florida.

There have been only a few sightings of the **Jaguar** in the United States since the late 1940s, but this beautiful spotted cat once occupied a territory that included southeastern and central California, and southern Arizona, New Mexico and Texas. Attaining weights of up to 300 pounds, it is an extremely powerful and efficient predator. Because it preys on livestock, and its fur is of great value, the jaguar has been heavily reduced in numbers in its major range, which extends from Mexico into South America.

Three other cats with primary ranges south of the Mexican border, and which American varmint hunters likely will never see, are the **Ocelot, Jaguarundi** and **Margay.**

The ocelot is the largest of the trio, attaining weights of up to 40 pounds. The tawny-gold body is covered with lines of brown, black-bordered markings: rosettes, bars, rings and specks. Once fairly abundant in the range they occu-

pied in the United States, they preyed on small livestock, which prompted efforts at eradication. Habitat loss also contributed to their decline, as did hunting them for their pelts.

Ocelots are fully protected over their present range, which includes southern Oklahoma, southwest Arkansas, western Louisiana, Texas and a small corner of southeastern Arizona.

The long, slim jaguarundi weighs between 15 and 18 pounds, and appears in three color phases: all black, all gray, and russet with a white underside. When animals of different colors breed, the young may be of mixed hues.

The only places in the United States where they have been known to occur are extreme southern Texas and extreme southeast Arizona.

The last margay sighting in this country was in Texas in the mid-1800s, and less is known about this small, 5- to 7-pound cat than any of its relatives, even in its primary range from Mexico to Argentina. It is known that it has exceptional climbing ability, and can descend a tree headfirst, a feat the other cats can't accomplish. Margays are thought to be mostly nocturnal, with an extremely secretive nature which makes observing their habits very difficult.

HUNTING METHODS

One of the earliest forms of hunting bobcats for sport dates back to Colonial times when dog packs were used to pursue and tree them. It's an exciting way to hunt them that reached its peak of perfection with the use of the Kentucky foxhound. One of the main qualities required in a 'cat hound is a good nose, because this animal leaves less scent in its travels than any of the other cats. Bobcats are also extremely tricky when being trailed, often doubling back on their track. A bobcat will usually be treed by dogs, but occasionally they bay and give dogs a fierce fight.

Bagging one of these animals without dogs or

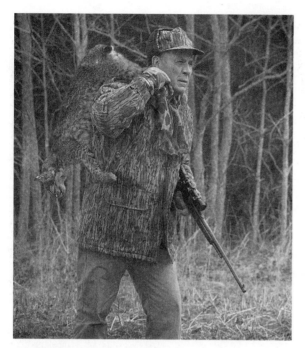

Many bobcats are killed incidentally by deer hunters. This one substituted for a buck on an Alabama hunt.

other devices can result in pretty slim pickings, and most bobcats taken under such circumstances are killed incidental to deer or turkey hunting. It's a case of two predators seeking the same prey at the same place.

If dog packs and incidental kills were the only way gun hunters could bag bobcats, the numbers they harvested would be quite small. However, there's another way to go about it that can pay big dividends, depending upon the skills of the individual involved: the use of predator calls.

Calling techniques that attract bobcats don't differ greatly from those used for other predators, except for the fact that the old saying about curiosity and cats applies. Calls unrelated to food often bring them in as quickly as ones that hold the promise of a meal. Too, because bobcats will make a run at prey many times larger than themselves, calling sounds don't have to be restricted to those emitted by the smaller creatures.

Calling techniques similar to those used for coyotes work equally well for bobcats. This team is hunting in South Dakota.

Double Buddy Bucket blind can accommodate a pair of hunters, allowing full concealment for both caller and shooter.

Also, the behavior of called bobcats is very unpredictable. Most of the time they approach cautiously, with the typical cat tactics of slow, deliberate movement, taking advantage of any type of cover available. They possess keen vision which is particularly acute at night since their eyes are designed to operate better in low light conditions; and their hearing is equally sharp. They depend mainly on these two senses; their sense of smell isn't particularly good. If the least bit suspicious, they either abandon the stalk and vanish, or stop and sit awhile to think things over. Patience is required on the part of the hunter because even if the animal stops, all isn't lost. Sometimes all it takes to get a bobcat interested again is to switch to another kind of call. If a nonfood kind brought it in, a mouse squeak or subdued rabbit distress call may do the trick.

Bobcats are shy and furtive, spending the daylight hours in dense cover sleeping or resting. They are mainly active at night, when they roam open areas seeking the rabbits and rodents that are the major part of their diet year-round. This is why night hunting is so much more productive for these animals. Bobcats can be called in the daytime, but they're so sneaky and elusive that they may be in close without the caller ever seeing them.

In scouting for bobcats, the best places to look for tracks and scat are along stream banks, around ponds or waterholes and in brushy or second-growth areas. Once enough sign is discovered to make a hunt feasible, the next step is to find the closest open space where you can set

Brell-Mar 5-pole blind is light and portable, and can be erected in minutes when you find a good place to set up.

The Huntin' Stump, made by API Outdoors, is extremely effective in the woods as a calling station for bobcats.

up to hunt after nightfall. Ideally, you want a spot without any cover so that you can see the bobcat as it approaches. Otherwise, the cats may come and go without your ever being aware of their presence. It also helps to have some elevation, whether it be the back of the truck, a tree or a natural rise in the terrain, since this makes it easier to spot a bobcat sneaking in. There's a particular satisfaction in bagging bobcats, mainly because of their reputation for stealth. But these predators are no more difficult to lure than any of the others.

EQUIPMENT AND ACCESSORIES

Both rifles and shotguns can be used on bobcats. The choice sometimes depends on whether or not you want to keep the pelt. A rifle will put a single hole in the hide, whereas a shotgun will make it a sieve.

One of the favorite bobcat cartridges is the .243 Winchester, but the .25-06 Remington and 6mm Remington are also popular. The smaller .22 centerfires like the .222 Remington and .223 Remington are very effective, too, but anything below this level ballistically isn't recommended. As for shotguns, a 12 gauge loaded with No. 4 buckshot is quite sufficient. Bobcats are tough creatures, and nobody wants to tangle with a crippled one. Those familiar with these animals realize that the old saying referring to a man who can "whip his weight in bobcats" meant that a *very* formidable person was being discussed.

Accessories are much the same as those used for hunting coyotes and foxes.

10

Crows

The crow is a member of a family that also includes ravens, jays and magpies, all bold, aggressive birds whose behavior ranges from simply annoying to highly destructive. The crow occupies the latter category. That's why it's a target for varmint hunters.

The **Common Crow** occupies almost all of North America except the far northern regions. It breeds from Newfoundland south to Florida and west across Canada, and winters across the United States and south into Mexico and beyond. In areas with moderate climates, crows don't migrate.

Crows are present almost everywhere—forests, fields, parks and suburban areas. Seeing them in inner-city areas is not uncommon. They operate from central positions, large roost sites at which they gather in late afternoon, following travel lanes back from wherever they have been feeding during the day. These roosts may harbor thousands of birds, and they're favorite locations at which gunners can waylay them. Shortly after dawn they are back on the move again, usually using the same travel lanes as they radiate over the countryside.

As omnivorous birds, crow eat almost any-thing: all kinds of vegetable, insect and animal matter, including carrion. Garbage dumps attract crows, and they have a great fondness for field crops.

Crows do extensive environmental damage. One of the most prominent examples is their severe impact annually on waterfowl populations. It's proof of how ruthlessly destructive these birds can be. When the hens begin laying, the crows invade the nests and break open and eat the eggs. Later, when the hatches occur, they devour the fledglings. The degree of devastation is incalculable, but it's obvious it significantly decreases the number of birds that migrate down the flyways each fall.

Crows take a heavy toll on upland-game birds and songbirds in the same manner, and they also prey on the young of small-game animals, such as rabbits and squirrels. Few predators can match them when it comes to destroying wildlife. Every hunter has witnessed crows being harassed in flight by smaller birds, which is evidence that they are regarded as natural enemies.

Like the coyote, the crow possesses a highly developed mentality, and experts say it has reached the highest stage yet achieved by any avian species. They have a solid social organization and a communication system that is both complex and extremely effective, attributes that help explain the crow's wariness and cunning. They also possess great predatory skills. In many ways this raucous, bold thief is a feathered version of its canine counterpart in environmental crime.

There are other things these two varmints share. Both have been the target of massive efforts aimed at their eradication. They have been poisoned, their roosts bombed, bounties placed on them and intense gunning pressure applied, yet they have endured. Due to changes in agricultural practices and other factors, crow populations across the country aren't as large as they once were; but they're plentiful enough to afford varmint hunters lots of shooting. There used to be no closed season on crows anywhere in the country, but now the U.S. Fish and Wildlife Service has ruled that each state must establish a closed season during the nesting period.

The crow's intelligence has given rise to many myths, one of which is that crows "hold court" and judge individual members of the clan for misdeeds. Some also believe that they descend upon offenders found guilty and either kill them or drive them away.

They do display other "smart" characteristics, though. Sometime sentinels are posted to watch fields in which they are feeding, and there's evidence that scouts are sent out in advance of feeding forays to check for danger. Crows also will drop clams, oysters or other hard-shelled prey on rocks to break them open, and they drop hickory and black walnuts on highways and let passing vehicles do the cracking.

The practice of "mobbing" hawks and owls has long been observed, and often large numbers of birds participate in these attacks on their enemies. What is sometimes mistaken for mobbing of an individual crow is nothing more than the other birds attempting to rob it of some choice food item it has obtained. It's a sort of aerial hijacking.

The crow also has a rather special distinction. During World War II it was designated as an enemy of the American public and was the subject of a widespread propaganda campaign. The message was that these "black bandits" were robbing the nation's farms of grain that was vitally needed for the production of food for both civilians and the military. Hunters were urged to destroy crows at every opportunity as a contribution to the war effort; and spurred on by patriotism, they went at it with a vengeance. Farmers had the priority in purchasing the limited supply of shotgun shells and .22 cartridges allotted to sporting goods and hardware stores.

There's no way to gauge the result of this crusade, but it's doubtful that its impact on the crow population was significant. Most of the men who were active hunters were in the armed forces, so the number of people participating in the extermination attempt wasn't massive, by any means. After the war, the crow population was more than adequate to keep hunters actively involved in the sport. What the wartime campaign mainly did was to briefly focus attention on a sport that had been practiced since the late 1800s when shooting these pesky birds became popular.

In the early years when agriculture was the major part of the nation's economy, conditions were ideal for supporting large crow populations. Huge numbers of the birds were present in some locations, especially in the farm belt states. At such places, some of the roosts attracted hundreds of thousands of crows. Shoots with lots of participants were often held at these sites, resulting in big kills, but even two or three hunters could count on bagging as many as several hundred birds in a day. There were, and still are, crow shooting contests held, with the winners eventually competing in a world championship. The interest isn't as intense as in years past, but the devotees are just as enthusiastic. Crow hunting is a special kind of sport, and there will always be hunters who eagerly accept the challenges they offer.

There are two other kinds of crows in North America, but both have very restricted ranges. Neither poses the environmental threat of the common crow, since their numbers are much smaller.

The **Fish Crow** inhabits seashores, estuaries, and large river valleys from New England to Florida and around the Gulf Coast to Texas. Its main source of food is fish, shoreline jetsam and various plants and berries found in the areas.

On the other side of the continent, the **Northwestern Crow** occupies a thin strip of range from Washington to Alaska. It occasionally feeds on croplands, but more often it scavenges along the seashores to obtain most of the items it eats.

HUNTING METHODS

A beginner who is considering taking up crow shooting as a sport must first realize that, like many other forms of hunting, it isn't as simple as it might seem. Crows are deceptive, and just because they don't seem to be especially wary when approached *without* a gun doesn't mean they're easy targets. As indicated, crows are extremely intelligent birds that always seem to be well aware of the intentions of people who come near them. Veteran hunters swear that they can tell the difference between a hand-held farm or garden implement and a gun. Some also believe that crows can count, so if four hunters enter a blind and two leave, the birds don't let their guard down. They know two are left inside. There's no absolute proof of this, but considering all of the other sophisticated faculties crows possess, it's worth thinking about.

Successful crow hunting is a combination of several factors, and while certain ones may seem more significant than others, they're actually highly interdependent. Put together properly, they're consistently unbeatable.

With this in mind, regard what follows as having nothing to do with levels of importance.

Calling

The vast majority of crow hunters are shotgunners who rely on calling to lure the birds. It's true that a rank amateur can attract their attention, and perhaps even knock some down, but it takes an expert to conduct a shoot that accounts for hundreds of birds.

The way to begin is at a sporting goods store, where you select a crow call which is accompanied by an instructional tape or video. This will allow you to learn all of the basics before going into the field. Then go to a place that crows frequent, hear how they "talk," and go home and try to mimic the sounds. The ones to which you should pay the most attention are the hail calls and those that indicate excitement or alarm.

Better still, go with a veteran crow hunter or team of hunters and listen to their repertoire of calls. These are the ones that are essential to successful crow hunting, since they're the ones that lure in, excite and hold birds.

No doubt calling was originally done by mouth, and while there are still many hunters who can display this talent, nobody disputes that greater efficiency and volume are produced by the manufactured kinds. These are reed-type calls, and while there are a great many models and styles on the market, they are basically the same. It all comes down to a matter of individual preference.

Crow calling is an art, and becoming proficient takes a lot of time and hunting experience. Crows can be easy to call one day and difficult the next, and calling repertoires should match different locations and situations. There's no single routine that can be used in all circumstances, and that's part of the challenge hunters face each trip into the field.

Mouth calls are the most widely used lures for hunting crows.

Individual calling can be effective, but a pair of hunters, or even a trio, can create a clamor that is more compelling. Teams that have been working together for a long time have individual roles, so even though they're calling in unison, the sounds they make aren't the same. The idea is to make crows think they're hearing a chorus of excited and angry voices.

Two calls are *musts*: the fighting call that represents angry crows that have come upon an enemy and are furious. It is one that should be performed with much gusto, because this gets crows within hearing all fired up and ready for combat. The madder they get, the better the results.

The second call is the hail or comeback call that's used to lure birds that have strayed away back into the fray. This call should be sounded as soon as any birds begin to leave. They're vulnerable until they get a distance away and begin to cool off a bit.

Once a response is elicited, hunters must keep their eye on the birds and watch how they respond, and then make little alterations in their calling to keep them coming. As crows approach, the tempo is increased in order to build them into full frenzy, ready to take on whatever enemy is present. Having dozens of crows swirling overhead is the culmination of this kind of effort.

Since crows are loud and aggressive by nature, calling must match these characteristics. Don't hesitate to put everything into it, because there's no way you can out-shout these loud-mouths. Most important is to establish a rhythm to build excitement and never pause.

One of the greatest boons to crow hunting was the development of the electronic call, which duplicates the sound of actual crow fights and clamor. These devices first appeared in the late 1950s and immediately became

Electronic calls are also very effective for crows. Here a hunter places a speaker outside his blind.

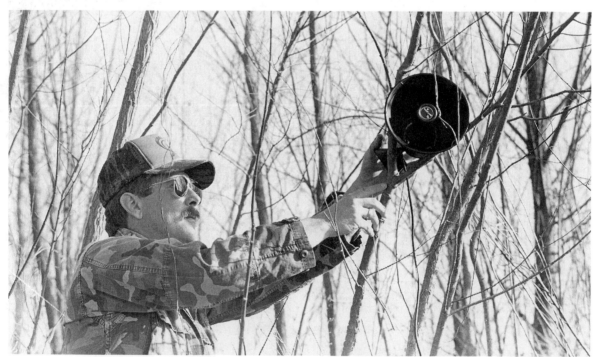

This hunter is placing a speaker in a tree at some distance from his blind in order to divert the crows' attention.

popular among hunters. They not only did a terrific job of attracting crows but also permitted both hands to be free at all times. The first models were simply portable phonographs that were large and cumbersome, but over the years there have been dramatic improvements in both the size of the units and sound quality. One of today's electronic calls is computerized and pocket-size, and it can be programmed to play a variety of calls for different conditions.

These innovations didn't replace the old methods, by any means. Many hunters didn't wish to abandon the thrill and sense of accomplishment derived from standard calling procedures. To them it was turning their backs on skills that had taken years to perfect and which gave them a lot of satisfaction. Also, electronic calls can't match traditional-style calling when it comes to versatility. There are many different situations encountered in crow hunting which require particular calling tactics, and in some of them it's necessary to shift quickly from one to the other.

Some hunters use both types of calls. A common tactic is to attract the crows with standard mouth calls, then turn on the electronic call when the birds start to approach. From that point they can keep on calling if they wish to supplement the other sounds, or just get ready to shoot.

Decoys

Once you've mastered calling, it's time to understand the use of decoys.

Feather-Flex great horned owl decoy (left) represents one of the crow's most hated enemies, and it's a sure-fire lure when accompanied by good calling. An owl decoy and a few crow decoys (right) are sufficient to produce some lively shooting.

The keys to successful crow hunting are effective camouflage and steady calling.

A typical hunting setup includes an owl perched in a stand or in a tree, surrounded by crow decoys both in the trees and on the ground. Crows attack all raptors, but especially great horned owls. Most hunters who have spent a lot of time in the woods have witnessed crows harassing hawks or owls. Obviously, these birds raid crow nests, but whatever the reason may be, there's the equivalent of a blood feud between them.

Once approaching crows see an owl decoy, it's all over but the shooting. They will zero in on the predator and make swooping passes at it that give the hunter choice, close-range shots. When the birds are sufficiently aroused, they don't seem much bothered by the gunshots, especially if the hunters continue to call.

While it isn't a common practice today, hunters have used live owls tethered to a platform atop a pole erected at the hunting site. In some instances another natural enemy of the crow—a tomcat—has been used in the same way.

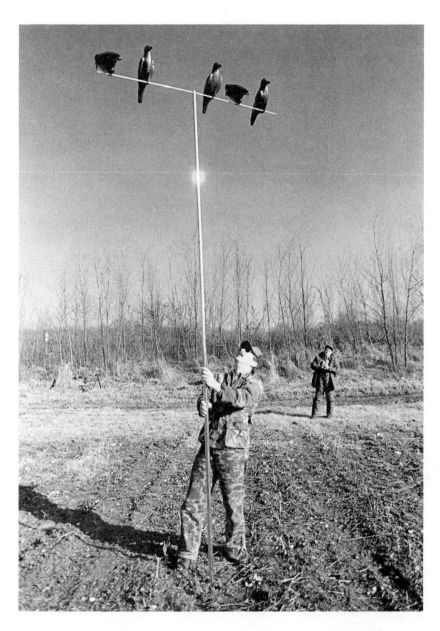

This Feather-Flex decoy "tree" can be placed in the open to give crows a better view of the decoys.

Once a few crows have been downed, they can be added to the decoys on the ground to make a more impressive spread. It's ordinary to have waves of crows coming to calls, allowing any blind or decoy adjustments to be made during lulls in the action.

Crow decoys can be as simple as profiles fashioned from plywood or cardboard and painted flat black. A stick can be attached to push into the ground and support the silhouettes. These work all right, but they're one dimensional and can't be seen by birds directly overhead.

The better decoys are full-bodied, some cast in a hard plastic or fiber, and others that are made of a soft plastic and are light and flexible. It's important that some decoys in each set have a clothespin or other fixture that will attach them to tree limbs or barbed-wire fences. The owl is always placed well above ground level, and it's best to have some decoys in the immediate area around it.

Sometimes half a dozen decoys are enough,

but having up to a couple dozen makes the scene even more compelling in the eyes of the crow.

Camouflage Clothing

Camouflage clothing is absolutely essential for successful crow shooting, and it should be as complete as possible. That means head-to-toe coverage, including hands and particularly the face. A naked face flashes like a mirror in the light, and it can spook crows from as much as a quarter to half mile away. Their eyesight is much keener than that of humans, and any little flaw in a setup can spell disaster. Many times

crows will send a single bird to a calling site to scout the area. It usually passes out of gun range, and if everything is right it returns to give the okay to the others.

Crows detect color very well, so this is a situation where red or blaze-orange caps and other visible, brightly colored accessories have to be avoided.

Face masks bother some shooters, in which case camouflage greasepaint can be substituted. This same substance can be applied to the hands if gloves are also a hindrance. A camouflaged shotgun provides the final touch in becoming invisible.

When there's snow on the ground, crows are easy to spot. Here a hunter gets set to fire at a crow feeding nearby.

Blinds

Special attention must be paid to blinds, because regardless of how well camouflaged the hunter may be, it's almost impossible to perform satisfactorily without additional concealment. When a couple or more hunters are involved, a blind supplies a central spot from which to operate and call.

At times, blinds can be fashioned from material found on the spot, but usually this takes a lot of time. The commercial blinds are better.

Blind placement is a key factor in bagging birds. It shouldn't be placed under trees since the branches will obscure overhead shots. Set it up in cover fairly near the decoys, making sure it's no higher than the vegetation in which it's placed. Otherwise it will stand out and crows will detect it.

Blinds should be placed a little upwind of the flyways crow use when they leave their roosts. If the wind shifts, change the position of the blind so you are still using it to your best advantage. That's one reason why it's advisable to use portable blinds. An alternative is to build several blinds at the location just to be sure you're backed up in case wind direction changes.

Setting up

Finding the best places to shoot crows requires some scouting and inquiries. A roost is a principal clue, because once you know their evening destination, it's rather simple to identify the major flyways on which they travel when fanning out over the countryside in the mornings. The places they have chosen to feed may be many miles away, and it's not necessary to know where these are. If you happen to be at one of them, all the better. It's important to position yourself somewhere along a flyway so you'll be certain of being able to see and hear the birds. Crows may be on their way to breakfast, but they seldom pass up the opportunity to join in what they perceive to be a brawl underway.

The same thing doesn't hold true in the evening when they're returning to the roost. Calling may cause a few birds to deviate from their path, but it's seldom that a high degree of excitement can be generated. Pausing takes time, and when the light is failing, they're anxious to get situated in the roost before darkness falls.

Roving hunters can almost always find spots where a quick setup will result in action, although the chances of collecting more than a dozen of so birds is usually minimal. This hopscotch method is useful when there's no hotspot available. Ride along back roads, stopping occasionally to call. A strong response can often signal the presence of crows looking for a fight, which can become a little bonanza for the hunters.

Crow silhouette decoys are effective when placed in the open to simulate feeding birds. This is a good tactic when hunting with a rifle

Wingshooting

Few sports are better for training a person in wingshooting techniques than crow hunting. First of all, you get the chance to do plenty of shooting, and some of the birds don't pose much of a challenge. Those are the "starters" that help build confidence, but on the other end of the spectrum there are the fast, tricky, birds that perform aerial maneuvers that can baffle even veteran gunners. Wind gives them even more of an advantage, because their large, powerful wings and broad "rudder" tail permits them to do amazing things. They can sail, hover, plummet like a rock, flare wildly, do snap rolls or use a tailwind to flash past a hunter at speeds resembling a jet fighter on a strafing run. Once witnessed, these aerobatics will inspire respect in any wingshooter.

Some of the toughest crow shooting is at roosts. Usually a number of hunters gather around a site in late afternoon and wait for the birds to arrive. They don't use calls or decoys. The birds, when they arrive, concentrate on settling into the trees before nightfall, and shooting doesn't deter them. Often the roost sites are in pine thickets, and with crows swirling overhead and diving into the roost from all directions, the action is fast and furious. It's almost as if the hunters are protecting the site against attacking birds. Since this begins to occur shortly before dark, it doesn't last long, but it's an unforgettable gunning experience. Because of the short-range shooting, this is one situation in which an improved cylinder bore will get the best results.

Rifles for Crows

Yet while the shotgun is the principal crow-hunting weapon, there's a fraternity of varmint hunters who prefer to use rifles to pick off the birds at long range. This doesn't provide the same hot-and-heavy action, but that's not what's expected. Hunters shoot at ranges between 200

and 300 yards with high-intensity cartridges such as the .220 Swift or .22-250 Remington.

This is a relaxing form of hunting, and a favorite way to go about it is to cruise back roads and spot birds sitting in trees or feeding in fields. In places where it's legal to shoot from vehicles, the hunter doesn't even have to expose himself. Crows aren't spooky about cars or trucks, but once a human form emerges, they go on full alert. Those who hunt in this manner often have rifle rests and spotting scopes mounted on the doors so no outside setups are needed. Shooting across the hood or top of a car, resting the rifle on sandbags, is a common practice. Care must be taken that the muzzle of the rifle is positioned so the blast doesn't scar or burn the paint.

There are certain times that are especially good for picking off crows with this tactic. They like to scrounge in newly plowed ground for worms and grubs, and they can also be counted on to be there whenever grain is being planted. Another prime time is just after a snowstorm when the ground is covered. Crows are very active when searching for food, and they're very easy to spot. If you can locate manure piles, you have a winner, because these are natural magnets for the birds.

One of the main challenges is that crows on the ground are usually walking or hopping around most of the time. A bird will stop just long enough for the shooter to get the crosshairs on it, then move just as the trigger is being squeezed. They're tough enough targets at long range without this kind of frustration. It's a good test of patience!

Decoys work well for riflemen, but the strategy is different. Sometimes hunters simply place a few crow decoys in a field that would normally attract the birds. Other times they set a great horned owl decoy on a post or in a small tree along a fence line. In either of these situations, calling can be helpful, but since the shooter will be sitting a couple of hundred yards behind the decoys, the only purpose is to get their attention initially. Once they spot the decoys, calling should be discontinued because the distance between the caller and the decoys can cause confusion.

Plenty of crows can be killed using this technique, and as evidence, consider the case of Ray Weeks, of Tillsonburg, Ontario. His feats with a rifle are mentioned in Harvey Donaldson's classic benchrest and varmint shooter's book, *Yours Truly*, recently reprinted by Wolfe Publishing Company.

Donaldson states that during the middle 1930s, Weeks managed to bag between 4,500 and 5,000 crows *every season*! He worked for an insurance company, and his job was to drive around Ontario collecting payments. Most of his travels were in rural areas, and by carrying a rifle and ammunition with him at all times, he had lots of shooting opportunities. Donaldson says Weeks used the .22 Hornet, chambered for his 2-R case, and the .219 Donaldson to attain his best records. The odds are very much against totals like that ever again being achieved, but the anecdote may inspire some readers to give rifle hunting for crows a second thought.

Another productive approach is to find places along the morning flyways where some crows leave the flight and begin foraging for food. The shooters wait for the birds to land on the

The payoff. A crow bagged at 150 yards when it and some others flew in to join the decoys on the ground.

ground or in a tree and then commence firing.

Finally, there are those who prefer to stalk crows with a rifle using the basic .22 rimfire cartridge. This is similar to squirrel hunting. The hunter sneaks through the woods and looks for crows sitting in trees. A call can be used to good effect, either to lure birds or to determine their location. Many youngsters have bagged their first crows this way.

EQUIPMENT AND ACCESSORIES

A 12-gauge shotgun is by far the most favored by crow hunters, because it is the most dependable killer. This gauge puts out a larger shot pattern than the 16 or 20 gauge, and it has greater range. Equipped with a set of choke tubes, it's practical for any situation, from high-flying birds that require full-choke patterns to birds that are diving in and coming within twenty-five yards. Modified or improved cylinder chokes are best for the task.

There are those who favor 16- and 20-gauge guns, but few who go so far as to recommend the smaller .410 and 28 bores. Crows aren't hard to kill, but sometimes the ranges work against the smaller-gauge guns and the amount of lead they throw.

Both low-brass and high-brass shells are okay, and shot sizes from No. 4 to No. 8 will do the job. Crows aren't hard to knock down, so smaller shot provides denser patterns. Many hunters use up shells from the previous hunting seasons, which may include a wide variety of loads.

Crows are tough to kill, so a 12-gauge shotgun is recommended. Four good crow guns are, left to right: Ruger Red Label over/under; Mossberg 3½-inch Magnum pump; Winchester 1400 automatic; and Winchester 1300 pump.

Dedicated crow hunters burn up a lot of ammunition, so it's not surprising that a lot of them reload their shells. One big shoot with store-bought ammunition shells can be pretty costly; and even with reloading, it's not cheap!

There are two major manufacturers of electronic calls, and both can create about every kind of crow sound that's ever been heard. One unit is worn on the belt and plays tiny phonograph records, but because of its limited volume, it's more practical for other varmints than crows.

Calls and camouflage have been covered earlier in this chapter.

There are times when insect repellant or the impregnated mesh clothing mentioned in the chapter on squirrel hunting can be very useful in areas where mosquitoes, deer flies or other biting bugs abound.

There are several pop-up-type blinds available. One fits into a bucket which also doubles as a seat. There are several shooting ports in the material. There's also a double version that accommodates a pair of hunters. These offer total coverage of the hunter and are snug havens from wind and rain.

One of the simplest blinds consists of a long length of camouflage cloth or mesh-plastic material with several long steel or aluminum poles that can be placed in the ground to establish a preferred configuration. The material is then put in place. The whole operation can be performed in minutes. These are light, easily portable and can be quickly moved.

Nothing beats a good set of binoculars when it comes to locating concentrations of crows or cataloging their flyways. They also permit a hunter to watch distant birds and determine their reaction to calls.

Long stays in a blind can be made more comfortable with either a light shooting seat or a cushion. There are many varieties made especially for hunters, camouflage and all.

A couple of large plastic trash bags will be helpful, because considerate hunters will sack up the dead birds, empty shells, shell boxes and any other debris in order to leave the shooting site unlittered. The degree of courtesy that's exhibited by varmint hunters on private property often determines whether a return invitation will be issued, but the same practice should be followed on public lands, as well.

11

Other Varmints

As mentioned earlier, sometimes there's no exact set of guidelines to determine what is and is not a varmint, but one thing is certain: there are literally dozens of birds and animals that definitely can be placed in this category.

Some of these are found throughout the country, while others occupy more restricted ranges. However, because of the overall abundance and distribution of many of the species, it can be safely said that there's no place in North America where there's not at least one varmint available at any time of the year. The examples already listed would probably cover that claim, but there are plenty more to consider.

It is worth mentioning again that the regulations applying to varmints differ from state to state and, in Canada, from province to province, and you should read the rules before going afield. In some instances, the species are under the jurisdiction of state laws, but others are protected under federal law. An example is the black-billed magpie, a destructive bird that plagues cattle and sheep ranchers in the western states. A 1972 amendment to the Migratory Bird Act of 1918 extended the blanket of pro-

tection to magpies, crows and some other species. Yet although crow hunting is still legal under loose seasonal restrictions, the magpie can be hunted only by persons holding a standing depredation permit. This essentially eliminates varmint shooters from the picture unless the farmers and landowners in possession of a permit happen to enjoy the sport.

Exempted were three birds, each an exotic, and all of which are abundantly distributed throughout the country.

It would be hard to say which is the most familiar, but one stands out as the best sport for varmint shooters: the **Domestic Pigeon**.

There are few faster or trickier birds than the pigeon, and even though the majority of them are city dwellers, there's plenty of opportunity to hunt them on farms. Sometimes the birds reside on the property, living in barns and other outbuildings, but urban pigeons often fly into the countryside to feed when grain is being planted or at harvest time. Landowners have little use for these pests, and there's usually no trouble in gaining permission to shoot them.

Pigeon shooting can be fast and furious, and

these birds can perform aerial maneuvers that would cause a jet pilot to turn green with envy. They're not easy to down, either, and most gunners go after them with 12-gauge shotguns and either beefed-up field loads or high-brass shells. Another bonus is that they're good to eat, but because they have long life spans and can be tough, it's best to parboil them before beginning the final cooking process.

Calls don't work on pigeons, but decoys get good results, and there are commercial models available. Place them in a field, then add dead birds to the set to make it more attractive. The main feeding periods are from early-to-mid morning and mid-to-late afternoon. There's no season or limit imposed.

The **Starling** is one of the most annoying and numerous of all North American vermin, yet few hunters go after them. It's a missed opportunity, since starlings can provide excellent wingshooting. When the spring and fall migrations are underway and millions of birds are on the move, a hunter can take a stand beside a tree or on a hilltop and practice those shots that are troublesome during bird season. It beats skeet or trap shooting in terms of versatility, and it's also a great way to teach a youngster to swing, lead and follow through on flying targets.

The **English Sparrow** used to be a major pest in urban areas, but with the passing of the horse as a means of conveyance, their numbers decreased rather dramatically. The birds depended upon horse manure as a major food source, and once this wasn't available, the population levels dropped. They are still nuisance birds and quite unimportant to adult varmint hunters, but they're significant, just the same. For many generations English sparrows were the first "game" young would-be hunters equipped with BB guns went after. As such they deserve mention,

Starling

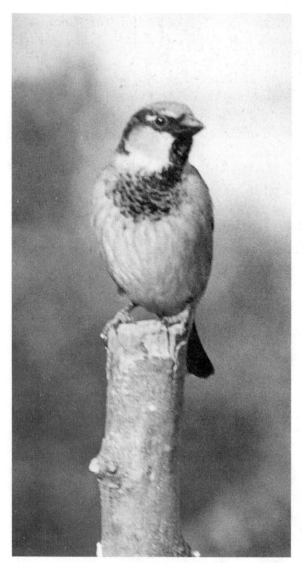

English Sparrow

because they served a very useful purpose. Perhaps in some places, they still do.

Throughout the entire country, but particularly in the midwestern and northwestern regions, there are a great number of **Weasels, Ground Squirrels, Chipmunks, Pocket Gophers, Rats, Mice** and **Voles** that can be legally hunted and which provide varmint shooters with an immense amount of shooting opportunity. It's not wasted, either. In some of the mid-continent states, these little critters, some of which are nicknamed "picket pins"

because of their upright stances, supply a large percentage of the activity. Like prairie dogs, most of these animals are very prolific, so there's seldom any shortage of targets. Only a very few of the species are protected, the black-footed ferret being the most prominent example.

Some varmint hunters prefer these small targets that require extreme accuracy. They're also good for educating young hunters, because they can be shot at either short or long ranges, the full gamut of calibers and cartridges can be used. The .22 rimfire is a good starter, but even veteran shooters often continue to include the

Pellet handguns and rifles are sufficient for starlings, sparrows and small rodents. Top to bottom: Crosman .22 caliber pistol, Crosman .177 caliber pistol, Crosman .177 caliber rifle, Crosman .22 caliber rifle with 3×-9× Bushnell scope.

Richardson's Ground Squirrel

13-Lined Ground Squirrel

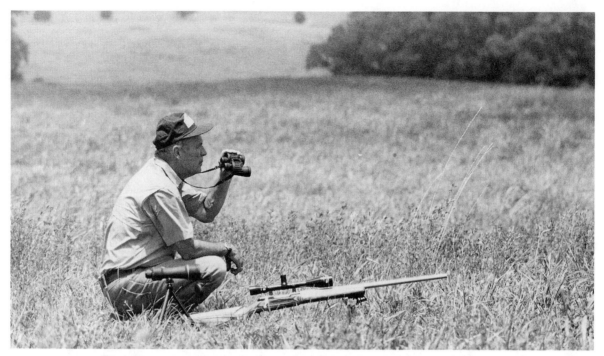

Shooting some of the small varmints at long range requires good optics and rifles that are extremely accurate.

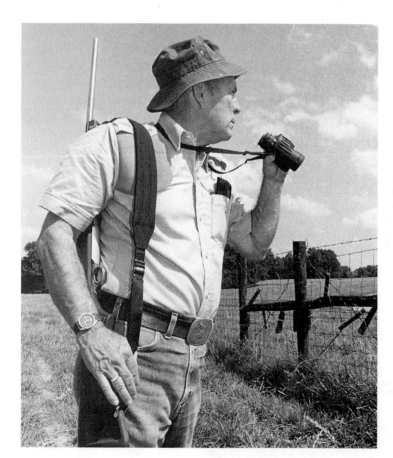

Roving is an enjoyable way to hunt small varmints.

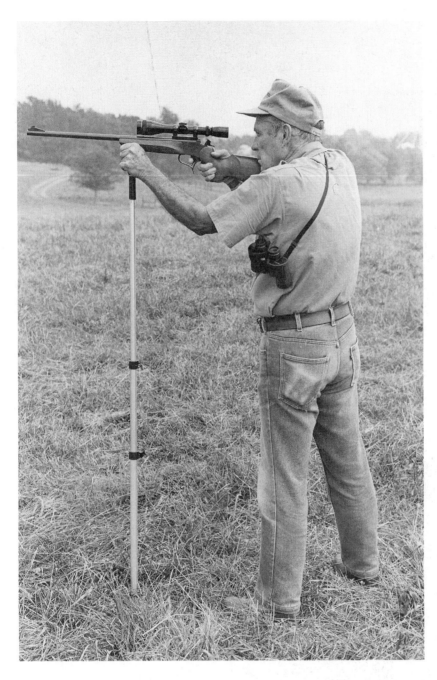

A telescoping camera monopod provides a handy rest for this Thompson/Center .17 caliber carbine with a 4× Leupold scope.

fancier, scope-equipped models in their stable of rifles used on the small varmints. This kind of hunting doesn't lend itself as well to long-range shooting as some of the others, mainly because the animals are too small to be seen at great distances. Cartridges with short to mid-range capabilities are better, which makes the .17 Remington and .218 Bee perfect picks for this sport.

The **Badger** is a tough, formidable burrower that is somewhat similar to the woodchuck, but with a much more aggressive and nasty temperament. They have flattened bodies and short legs, with a white stripe from the shoulder to the tip of their upturned nose, and white cheeks with a black patch. The coat is shaggy and grizzled brown or gray. The foreclaws are large,

Shooting ground squirrels off-hand with a rifle like this Ruger M77 in .22-250 or its equivalent is a real challenge.

enabling the badger to excavate earth at incredible speed. It weighs from 8 to 25 pounds.

Badgers feed mostly on small rodents and rattlesnakes. They often occupy the burrows they create when digging out their prey. Ranchers dislike these animals because of the danger their burrows pose to hoofed livestock.

Man is the badger's principal enemy, and they're still legally hunted and trapped in some places within their range, which includes most of the midwestern and western states and parts of the western Canadian provinces.

Badger

12

Firearms Safety

There is no way to overemphasize firearms safety. It is the most important part of hunting and shooting. Guns are lethal weapons and must be regarded as such. Yet guns, like cars, aren't the cause of accidents. *People* are, and this is why it's vital that everyone operating and handling them be fully competent and aware of the safety rules. Even the best trained and most responsible people have accidents. Among those who aren't, the incidence is vastly increased.

Ideally, firearms safety education should begin at home, because this is where more than 70 percent of the firearms deaths occur each year. People own guns for both personal protection and recreational purposes, and they are present in over 75 percent of the homes in the United States. Because of this, some of the rules of safety practiced in the field must also be observed in the home.

Courses in home firearms safety are available. Ask your state wildlife agency about them. The purpose is to educate people of all ages, especially children, of the dangers posed by guns.

Most youngsters, particularly boys, play with toy pistols or rifles, and unless otherwise instructed, often make no distinction between play guns and real ones. A home safety course will teach them lessons that will serve them well throughout their lives.

For example, they'll learn why it is important not to point guns at anyone. It's hard to enforce, since kids like to play games fashioned after what they see on television or in movies, much of which involves violence. It's worth the effort, though, and it can be effective if approached in a reasonable and diplomatic manner.

In the process, the dangers of *real* guns can be made clear, because it's quite possible they will be encountered sometime in one way or another. Responsible parents keep firearms safely locked away, but there are too many households where loaded guns are left in dresser drawers or other places of easy access. Curious or angry children can get hold of them, often with tragic consequences.

Unfortunately, both the media and the gen-

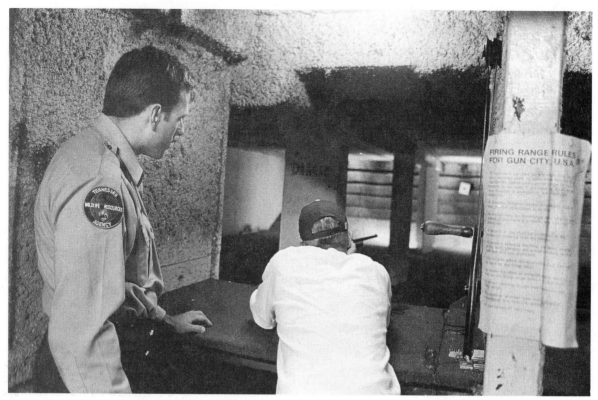

An instructor supervises a young shooter on his first visit to a rifle range. Hunter Education Programs are offered in every state.

eral public too frequently choose to place the blame on guns rather than on human error. In so doing, they portray guns as *bad*, and this negative impression must be overcome by those who teach youths.

Once the basics are covered, the best way to put children on the right track is to let them shoot at targets or plink with an air gun. That's the best way to convey the positive aspects of guns and shooting, by focusing on the fun and satisfaction of developing skills. And whether or not they eventually become hunters or shooters, they have been properly introduced to guns.

Early shooting training can be conducted in the home by using kits that provide everything necessary to help youngsters from eight to fifteen learn marksmanship and correct gun handling. This is a basic step that was first introduced by Daisy Manufacturing Company more than forty years ago as a part of the company's successful shooting education program for young people. This aggressive and successful endeavor has assisted in the training of millions of youngsters.

Also, for more than twenty-five years, Daisy and the U.S. Jaycees have co-sponsored a program that begins with grassroots shooting education classes and ends with the International BB Gun Championships. It attracts participants from all over the world. The cooperation has extended to other groups, and it now enjoys the sponsorship of the Boy Scouts of America, 4-H, National Rifle Association, National Guard, American Legion, and many other schools, camps, clubs and civic groups. There's plenty of opportunity available for kids to learn shooting and gun handling.

Once youngsters have been schooled in the

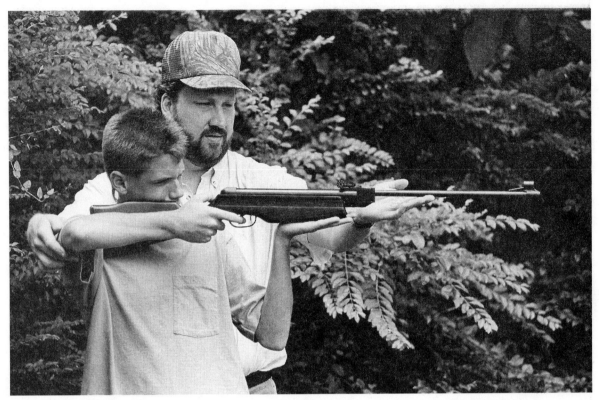

A young boy tries his hand at shooting Daisy's Power Line 130 with a little help from an instructor.

basics, the next step is to enroll them in the Hunter Education Program that is offered in every state. In almost all of them, it is mandatory that all young and new hunters possess a certificate of completion before being allowed to purchase a hunting license. As time passes, the percentage of hunters in the field who have received firearms training will steadily increase.

The first state-sponsored hunter safety program was offered in 1945, and the initial mandatory program began in 1949. Since 1978, hunter safety courses have been available in all 50 states, and more than 16 million youths have received instruction. Presently over 700,000 students get certificates each year.

Just as impressive, the Hunter Education Association reports that by 1988 the number of hunting-related fatalities had declined by 50 percent during a 30-year period. Much of this can be directly attributed to the hunter safety courses, since about 40 percent of the hunting accidents are caused by juveniles under the age of 21, and this is the age group directly targeted by the program.

While hunter education is aimed primarily at youths, many adults take the course, sometimes along with their sons and daughters. In some cases it's a refresher, but just as often it's the parent's initial exposure to information on firearms handling.

Although the fundamentals of gun handling, cleaning, shooting and marksmanship are vital, the course includes much more. Students are taught their responsibilities to themselves and others, to property owners and to the land itself. The basics of game management and wildlife identification are covered, as well as various problems a hunter may encounter in the field

Being safe in the field is important. This small distress signal kit is a valuable item to carry with you in the event of an accident.

that require special attention, such as hypothermia or snakebite. There are also tips on hunting, field dressing game and care of meat.

The full gamut of hunting weapons is covered: modern rifles, shotguns and handguns; muzzleloaders; bowhunting equipment; and the various kinds of ammunition and projectiles they utilize. There is even information on the safe operation of off-road vehicles, all-terrain vehicles and boats which hunters use as means of transportation.

There are many other safety courses offered throughout the country sponsored or sanctioned by reputable organizations, and all have value. Some are designed principally to instruct people on gun use for self or home protection, and these are also valuable. Anything that promotes more responsible and safe handling and care of firearms is welcome.

Many versions of The Ten Commandments of Firearms Safety exist, but all have essentially the same message. One of the most simply stated and understandable of these is the one produced by the National Shooting Sports Foundation:

1. Always keep the muzzle pointed in a safe direction.

This is the most basic gun safety rule. If everyone handled his firearm so carefully that the muzzle never pointed at something he didn't intend to shoot, there would be virtually no firearms accidents. It's as simple as that, and it's up to you. A safe direction means a direction in which a bullet cannot possibly strike anyone, taking into account possible ricochets, and the fact that bullets can penetrate walls and ceilings. Make it a habit to know exactly where the muzzle of your gun is pointing at all times, and be sure that you are in control of the direction in which the muzzle is pointing, even if you fall or stumble.

2. Firearms should be unloaded when not actually in use.

Firearms should be loaded only when you are in the field or on a target range or shooting area, ready to shoot. Firearms and ammunition should be secured in a safe place, *separate* from each other, when not in use. Unload your gun immediately when you have finished shooting, well before you bring it into a car, camp or home.

Whenever you handle a firearm, or hand it to someone, always open the action immediately, and visually check the chamber, receiver and magazine to be certain they do not contain any ammunition. Never assume a gun is unloaded—check for yourself! Never push or pull a firearm toward yourself or another person.

3. Don't rely on your gun's safety.

Treat every gun as though it can fire at any time, regardless of the pressure on the trigger. The "safety" on a gun is a mechanical device

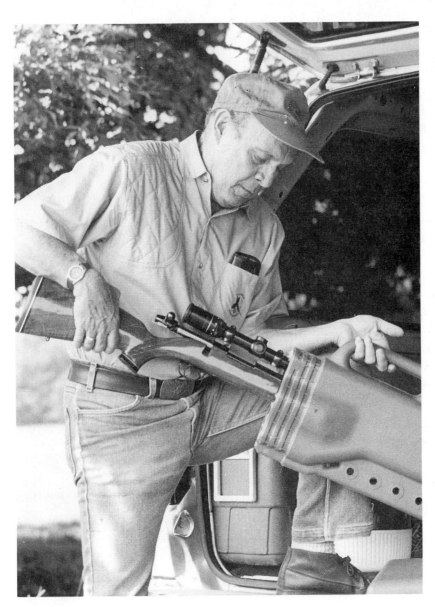

Kolpin's gun boot can be padlocked; it's a safe place to store a firearm.

which, like any such device, can become inoperable at the worst possible time. Besides, by mistake, the safety may be "off" when you think it's "on." The safety serves as a supplement to proper handling, but cannot possibly serve as a substitute for common sense. *Never touch the trigger on a firearm until you actually intend to shoot.* Keep fingers away from the trigger while loading or unloading.

4. Be sure of your target and what's beyond it.

No one can call a shot back. Once a gun fires, you have given up all control over where the shot will go or what it will strike. Don't shoot unless you know exactly what your shot is going to strike. Be sure that your bullet will not injure anyone or anything beyond your target. No target or animal is so important that you do not have the time before you pull the trigger to be absolutely certain of your target and where your shot will stop.

5. Use correct ammunition.

You must assume the serious responsibility of using only the correct ammunition for your firearm. Read and heed all warnings including those that appear in the gun's instruction manual and on the ammunition boxes. Improper or incorrect ammunition can destroy a gun and cause serious injury. Use only the ammunition that exactly matches the caliber or gauge or your gun.

6. If your gun fails to fire when the trigger is pulled, handle with care!

Occasionally, a cartridge may not fire when the trigger is pulled. If this occurs, keep the muzzle pointed in a safe direction. Keep your face away from the breech. Then carefully open the action, unload the firearm, and dispose of the cartridge in a safe way. Any time there is a cartridge in the chamber, your gun is loaded and ready to fire—even if you've tried to shoot and it did not go off.

7. Always wear eye and ear protection when shooting.

All shooters should wear protective shooting glasses and some form of hearing protection while shooting. Exposure to shooting noise can damage hearing. Adequate vision protection is also essential. Shooting glasses guard against twigs, falling shot, clay target chips and the rare ruptured case or firearm malfunction.

8. Be sure the barrel is clear of obstructions before shooting.

Before you load your firearm, open the action and be certain that no ammunition is in the chamber or magazine. Then glance through the barrel to be sure it is clear of any obstruction. Even a small bit of mud, snow, excess lubricating oil, or grease in the bore can cause dangerously increased pressures, causing the barrel to bulge or even burst on firing, which can cause injury to the shooter and bystanders.

9. Don't alter or modify your gun, and have guns serviced regularly.

Firearms are complicated mechanisms which are designed by experts to function properly in their original condition. Any alterations or changes made to firearms after manufacture can render the gun dangerous and usually void of any factory warranties. Do not jeopardize your safety or the safety of others by altering the trigger, safety or other mechanism of any firearm or allowing unqualified persons to repair or modify them. Your gun is a mechanical device which will not last forever and is subject to wear. As such, it requires periodic inspection, adjustment and service. Check with the manufacturer of your firearm for recommended servicing.

10. Learn the mechanical and handling characteristics of the firearm you are using.

Not all firearms are the same. The method of carrying and handling firearms varies in accordance with the mechanical characteristics of

Marlin gun-locking system is available for handguns, rifles and shot-guns. It's an excellent way to ensure the weapon cannot be fired.

The Savage lock system totally blocks the trigger mechanism.

Two models from Browning's line of gun vaults, one of the best ways
to keep firearms safely stored out of the reach of childern.

each gun. Since guns can be so different, no person should handle any firearm without first having thoroughly familiarized himself with the particular type of firearm he is using, the safe gun handling rules for loading, unloading, carrying and handling that firearm, and the rules of safe gun handling in general.

A couple of additional rules should be added:
Make absolutely certain that *all guns and*

ammunition be kept under lock and key in the home. Some people take a loaded gun out at night for protection, but it should be immediately locked up again in the morning.

Shooters who reload must exercise extreme caution and be sure all components are boldly and accurately marked. Gunpowder, percussion caps and anything else that could endanger children or others should be locked up.

13

Ethics

Ethics refer to moral standards, which in turn relate directly to how a person behaves. Taken one step further, ethics are closely linked to responsibility.

Each individual has a set of *personal* ethics, but in almost all areas of human activity there are also *stated* ethics. These spell out the rules of behavior that apply in a given situation.

Hunting is one of these areas, and while some of the rules of the sport are simply ethical do's and dont's, others are matters of *law*. Because of this, sometimes violation of the rules is more than unethical—it's illegal!

One of a hunter's first responsibilities is to be thoroughly familiar with the laws governing seasons, bag limits, legal hours, trespass laws, license requirements and any special regulations. Going afield without this knowledge will inevitably lead to violations, and the buck definitely stops with the guilty individual. A good hunter is a well-informed hunter.

Something else that must be remembered: hunters are under much more scrutiny by the general public than before, and examples of unethical or illegal activities generate heated criticism by various anti-hunting organizations. While the majority of Americans still favor hunting, the edge over those who consider it wrong isn't substantial. There are various reasons for their opposition, some which are focused on killing animals, and others that are mainly anti-gun arguments. Yet there is strong objection to the irresponsible acts of hunters. It's plain to see that those who commit these violations of either ethics or laws are enemies of the millions of responsible people who cherish the sport.

What many nonhunters fail to understand is that killing animals isn't the sole purpose of hunting. Many people prefer to eat wild game rather than commercially processed meat. To them, it is tastier; nutritionists have proved that it is healthier.

That's just one facet of the picture, and not always the most important. Just getting out and enjoying the outdoors is a great and satisfying

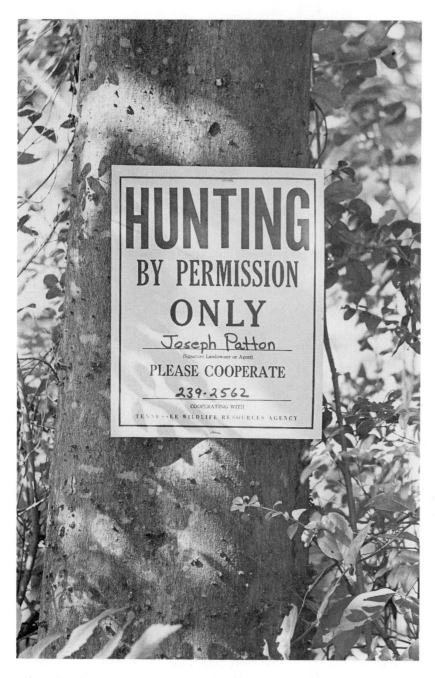

Responsible hunters always ask permission before hunting on private land. Sometimes, because varmint hunters do land-owners a favor, they get access to lands otherwise posted to all hunting.

pleasure. For example, tramping the fields on an October day with clear, blue skies, blazing leaf color and the scent of autumn is a matchless experience. For some, it also offers the opportunity to test their stalking, tracking or calling skills. Others like to view and photograph wildlife. And being afield with friends affords a kind of comradeship not found elsewhere.

Hunting is a heritage that's precious to those who participate, but like anything of great value, it must be protected.

PERSONAL RESPONSIBILITY

Every hunter is responsible for making each outing as safe and successful as possible. Small-game and varmint hunters aren't subject to some of the laws that apply to big-game hunters, particularly in regard to wearing blaze orange or other brightly colored cap or garment. However, rabbit hunters are advised to do so, since heavy cover can make it difficult to see companions, or for them to see you.

If going afield alone, it's wise to advise someone of where you will be hunting. That way, if an accident should occur, whether it be a physical injury or an automobile problem, you can be located. This can save a lot of worry on the part of family or friends, and sometimes it can be a lifesaver.

Mobile phones or radios can be useful in some situations. When two or more hunters are in the field together, small, compact walkie-talkie units assure contact.

Finally, a fanny pack or small day pack containing a first-aid kit, flashlight and emergency blanket can be an invaluable addition to your standard gear.

RESPONSIBILITY TO LANDOWNERS

Small-game and varmint hunters use private lands to a greater extent than do big-game hunters, so access to them is of great importance. The only way it can be maintained is by not only respecting the rights of landowners but also by establishing good personal relationships with them.

First of all, most states require hunters to have written permission before entering private land, and ordinarily signs posting the property state this. However, even if there are no posted signs, the law still applies. In other words, just because there are no "No Hunting" signs doesn't mean you can trespass.

Violation of this law by the few leads to consequences that affect all hunters. Much of the private land on which no hunting is allowed was so designated because of hunter abuses. No

one can blame landowners for taking such action, and in most cases there is no way to undo the damage.

When granted the privilege of hunting on private land, the individual must conduct himself properly and respect the landowner's conditions. The hunter should take care not to damage fences, leave gates open, shoot in the direction of farm buildings or livestock, damage crops, leave any sort of litter (including spent rifle or shotgun shells), or violate any of the game laws. Too, rabbit or squirrel hunters should offer to share some of the game with their host. It helps cement a relationship and open the door for future hunts.

Many hunters make visits to landowners well ahead of the season in order to get acquainted and request permission. This gives the landowner the opportunity to size up the individual and decide if he wants him as a guest. Sometimes this pay off very well, because for safety's sake, many landowners restrict hunting privileges to only a small number of people.

RESPONSIBILITY TO PUBLIC LANDS

Some of the lands most valuable to hunters are the state and federal forests, parks and refuges, since these belong to the public and are accessible to everyone. They are places a hunter can depend upon when no other hunting areas are available. Often these lands provide excellent hunting.

However, such lands serve many purposes, only one of which is hunting; so while they're available to hunters, they're not their exclusive domain. They also provide a variety of other recreational opportunities—fishing, camping, hiking, nature and wildlife photography—as well as being water sources for domestic and agricultural uses, lumbering and grazing lands.

One of the most common problems on these public lands is vandalism, and hunters often get

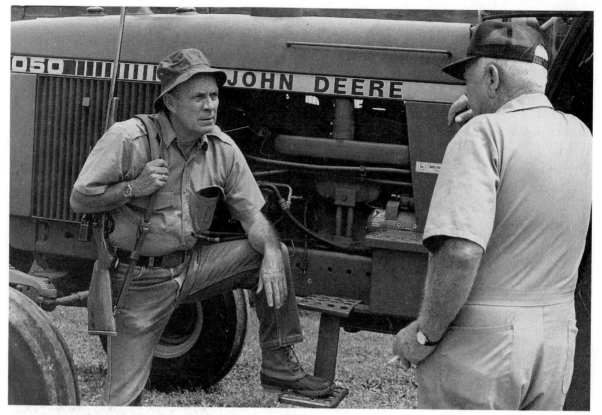

A hunter talks with a farmer about getting rid of some wood-chucks that have invaded his soybean fields.

the blame for some of the depredations. Shooting at signs is one, since it's easy to link this with hunters, even though other people may be responsible. Campground littering is rampant, as well as the accidental or deliberate setting of wildfires. The only thing hunters can do to offset bad impressions is to go the extra mile and set the best possible examples of proper behavior and respect for these invaluable public lands. Without them, everyone who loves the outdoors will suffer.

RESPONSIBILITY TO WILDLIFE

Whether the animal or bird being sought is game or varmint, it is the hunter's obligation to try to harvest it as cleanly and humanely as possible. This means that skill in shooting should be attained before going into the field, because inaccurate shots cause unnecessary crippling. Injured animals or birds often escape, only to die slowly or suffer for long periods. Sometimes this can't be prevented, but being proficient in the use of guns is important.

When crippling occurs, one of the other talents every good hunter should possess comes into play. Competence in tracking can make it possible to retrieve game that otherwise would be lost.

To achieve full competence in the field, it's essential to be very well informed about the quarry. This knowledge contributes to the success rate and enhances personal satisfaction. Hunting is a battle of wits, and if one doesn't understand the habits and behavior of the quarry, there's a good chance of coming up empty-handed.

Taking home game for the family to enjoy is

a bonus, yet just how flavorful it will be depends upon how it is handled after the kill. Care of game will be discussed in another chapter, but the point here is to recognize that mishandling game can make it unfit for consumption. Game should be seen as a prized possession and treated as such.

RESPONSIBILITY TO OTHER HUNTERS

Hunters can't always depend upon enjoying complete solitude, so the courtesy and respect extended to others who may be encountered in the field must be addressed.

First, you must remember that unless you happen to be the landowner, you may be *sharing* the hunting area. If so, it's a good idea to meet and discuss the best way to divvy up the territory. Trying to compete generally leads to spoiling the hunt for all involved and can end up in arguments and even fights.

Many times these meetings develop into friendships, some of which evolve into new hunting partnerships. Hunters are usually gregarious individuals, and when together there's ordinarily a high degree of compatibility. Visit any hunting camp and this will become apparent almost instantly.

The main thing is to have a positive attitude toward others in the field and to look out for their safety as well as yours. A hunter should not

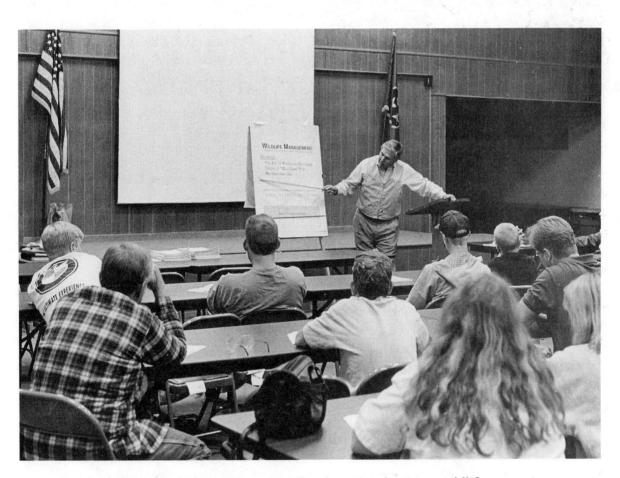

Many state game agencies provide education classes on wildlife management for both students and the general public.

intrude on other hunters' territory or disturb game in that vicinity. Cooperation with others in the field begins when someone extends a friendly or helping hand. A responsible hunter will not hesitate to initiate this process.

RESPONSIBILITY TO HUNTING LAWS

Hunting laws were established for the benefit of both hunter and wildlife. Without such regulations, each would suffer, and it would be realistic to assume that the sport of hunting could disappear forever.

There is a good basis for such a prediction. In the past, overhunting and lack of seasons and bag limits reduced some game birds and animals to near extinction, many of which have never recovered to the point where hunting them is feasible. It's obvious that some never will.

Game once flourished throughout North America, and there seemed to be an unending abundance. That was before the westward movement resulted in mass habitat destruction, which along with unregulated sport and market hunting seriously diminished the numbers of many of the species. The downward plunge continued until game laws were passed and management practices put into action. This came just in time for some species but too late for others.

Today, the supply of game available to hunters is proof that these laws and regulations have been successful. The populations of many wildlife species are now larger than ever before, and areas where certain animals had been decimated again have healthy numbers as a result of restocking programs.

These things would not have been possible without hunter cooperation and the dollars they spend for licenses. That's why respect for the laws and good ethics are vital.

14

Processing Game

In earlier days when most of the population was rural, wild meat was a very important part of the diet. Game was abundant and, with no restrictions, could be gathered at any time. Later when hunting seasons were established, it remained on the menu throughout the year. Farm women canned, pickled, dried or smoked game meat.

Usually, the happy chore of collecting squirrels and rabbits was assigned to young boys. Before school, after school and on weekends, these youths could be found afield with their single- shot .22 rifles or shotguns. Farm families were typically large, so this meant a concerted effort to gather as much game as possible. Few boys backed off from the challenge. It beat pitching hay and cleaning out barns by a mile!

Today, most hunters view the game they bag as a real bonus, and a special treat to be anticipated on the table. It can be a delicious and different addition to market meat, but only if it is properly handled and processed. Otherwise it will become unsuitable for consumption. Considering how negligent some hunters are in this department,

it's no wonder that many people complain of the "wild taste" of game they are served.

Processing game correctly is one of the skills every hunter should perfect; it is equally as important as some of the others necessary for success. A conscientious hunter doesn't waste game, and allowing it to become tainted as a result of mishandling is much the same as throwing it away. That's what is going to happen eventually, anyway.

One of the main things to remember is that the more quickly the meat is cooled, the better the flavor will be. Some places have squirrel seasons that begin early in the fall when temperatures are still very warm, and animals killed at these times should be gutted as soon as possible. Opening them up allows the heat to dispel much more rapidly. If this isn't done, the combination of body heat and air temperature will cause spoilage to begin within a very short time.

Even when cooler conditions exist, field dressing is still suggested. Often bullets or shot have penetrated intestines and allowed fluids to seep into the abdominal cavity. This can quickly

There are many knives and accessories that are useful in processing small game. Some models have tools included in one unit.

contaminate the meat, so getting rid of this possibility quickly is well worthwhile.

For field dressing small game, a big hunting knife is a disadvantage. A large blade isn't needed. The most useful knife is a small fixed-blade or folding model. Later, if the animal is to be skinned, a different choice of tools may be needed.

There's one exception to this. Rabbits can be field dressed *without* a knife by using a unique method of removing the intestines. It's done by grasping the animal just behind the front legs with one hand and squeezing hard. Then place the left hand below the right and compress the insides toward the rear so it protrudes to more than twice its normal circumference.

While maintaining a tight hold, raise the rabbit overhead and swing down hard like driving with a golf club. The pressure causes the lower

abdominal wall to tear, allowing the heart, lungs, liver and intestines to be thrown out. This takes care of the field dressing and lightens the load, since several rabbits can get heavy in a hurry! Incidentally, the heart and liver are very good to eat, so these items should be retained.

It isn't wise to place animals in plastic bags, since this will hold in body heat. Squirrel hunters often carry game on their belt, which permits plenty of air flow and more rapid cooling. Rabbit hunters can sometimes drop by their vehicle occasionally and put their game in the back of a truck or other open area.

Other than a knife, it's convenient to carry along a few paper towels. These can be used to wipe the body cavity dry after field dressing, and can be buried afterward. Another handy item is the little packaged, premoistened towels for cleaning the hands.

This Eze-Lap diamond sharpener is only 4 inches long before assembly, and can be carried in a leather belt pouch.

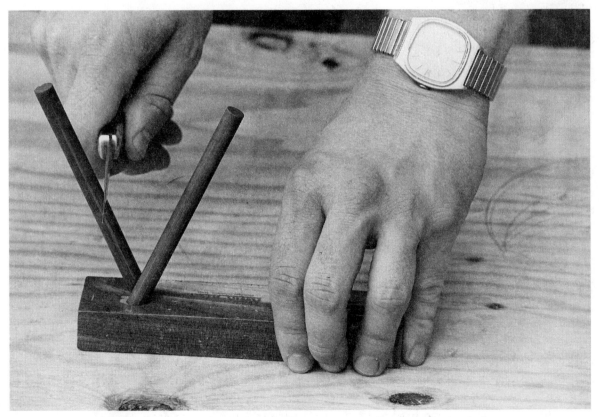

The Kwik-Sharp ceramic stick sharpener is a favorite for both large and small blades. Sticks are slanted at the correct angle.

SKINNING A SQUIRREL

1. First step is to make a 2- to 3-inch slit across the back.

2. Pull in both directions, much like peeling off sweat pants and shirt.

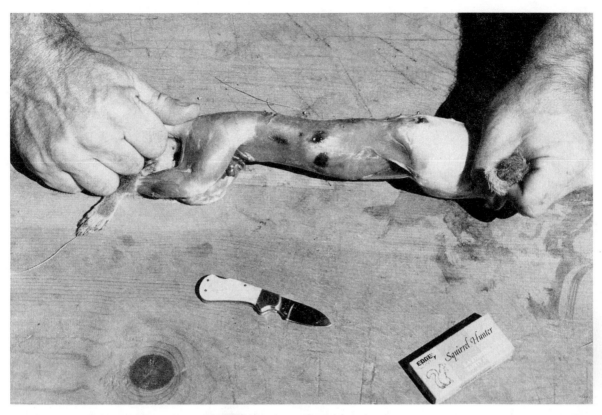

3. Skin out all but the last joint of the legs, the tail and head.

4. Finally, cut off the legs, head and tail, then remove the visceral material.

In order to keep the meat as clean as possible, it's better to wait until you're back home or in camp to skin animals. Leaving the hide on after field dressing doesn't hurt anything. Instead, it serves as a very suitable "wrapping." There are two schools of thought on the final job of skinning. Some hunters prefer to hang animals for a few days in a cool place before skinning; others like to complete this job as soon as possible. One thing to remember is that most small game animals have layers or pockets of excess fat. Take care to remove all of this, since it can adversely affect the flavor of the meat.

Following are what most hunters agree are the best ways to prepare game for the table.

SQUIRRELS

There are two ways to skin squirrels. Either one gets the job done in minutes.

The first requires only that a slit be made in the skin across the lower back that's wide enough to admit a couple of fingers of both hands. With the fingers hooked in each side of the opening, pull in opposite directions and the hide can be peeled off in seconds.

Once this is done, the head, feet and tail can be cut off. After that, the body can be cut into pieces, rinsed in cold water and placed in the refrigerator or prepared for cooking. Some hunters are fond of squirrel brains, and in this event, the head should also be skinned, cut off and added to the other edible parts.

The second approach is nearly as easy. Make a slit across the lower abdomen even with the anal opening, then cut through the tail, being careful not to sever the skin on the opposite side. Once this is done, take hold of the back legs, place your foot on the tail, and pull. The skin will come off from the hind quarters forward. Skin out the front and back legs (and the head, if desired).

Both of these methods work best on freshly killed squirrels, because the skin comes off much more easily. The longer you wait, the harder the task becomes.

RABBITS

The skin of rabbits isn't as tough as that of a squirrel, so it isn't as easily removed. However, the technique of making a slit across the back and pulling in opposite directions will work. The problem is that the skin sometimes tears, but if the animal is warm, it's no trouble to get it all off fairly quickly.

Skinning rabbits almost always results in a lot of hair clinging to the membrane that surrounds the flesh. This can be removed with a stiff brush while the carcass is being rinsed. If this doesn't work satisfactorily, a cloth dipped in scalding water will wipe away bits of fur that remain. This is a good procedure to follow with any small-game animal.

Rabbits sometimes carry tularemia, so as a precaution against infection it's wise to use rubber gloves while cleaning them. Otherwise, be sure to wash your hands thoroughly afterward with strong soap.

Many people believe that letting rabbits remain in the refrigerator for several days before cooking tenderizes meat. The best way to store it is in water with a little salt added.

RACCOONS AND OPOSSUMS

Throughout the ranges of both of these species there are plenty of people who consider both to be excellent table fare. Raccoons in particular have been popular, and there are places where the meat has been commercially marketed. Trappers got a double benefit from the animals by being able to sell both the fur and the carcass.

There's no quick and easy way to skin raccoons, so whether it's the meat or the hide that's important, the procedure is much the same. Essentially, this requires making a cut from the vent up the back of both hind legs to the last joint. Another cut is made from the anal vent to the base of the neck. A cut halfway around the tail will allow the center portion to be pulled out. Then simply work off the hide and pull it over the head to the nose, cutting off the feet in the process.

Under the front armpits (or legpits), and on either side of the spine are small "kernels" or scent glands that should be excised.

Much the same technique can be used on opossums, except that there are no scent glands to be concerned with, and even if the hide is to be retained, it's not necessary to save the tail.

When the animal is skinned and rinsed off, remove the fat and cut it into pieces unless it is to be baked whole. A few days refrigeration will probably help improve the quality. Unless the animals are obviously young, it's also wise to parboil the meat before final preparation. Old raccoons and opossums are very tough unless tenderized.

WOODCHUCKS

Woodchucks, especially young ones, are very fine eating, but getting the skin off the varmints is a tough chore. It has been said that the best way to accomplish it is "anyway you can," but employing the same basic techniques used with raccoons will do. The difficulty is that the hide and flesh seem almost welded together.

Experienced hunters make an effort to take care of their woodchuck needs by concentrating on picking off young animals in spring and early summer. That way the problem of having to parboil the meat is averted.

Once skinned, the scent glands should be removed and the animal cut up and soaked in a mild saline solution for a couple of days.

BEAVER

The meat of beaver is a sort of "sleeper," since few hunters think of it as table fare. However,

the meat is rich and very flavorful, and making an effort to harvest a couple of young animals can result in a culinary treat.

The standard skinning routine for all but squirrels and rabbits should be followed, and since the tail is regarded as gourmet fare by some people, it can also be skinned. There are castor glands at the base of the tail that should be removed, and while young animals seldom have much excess fat, get rid of any that's present.

For most recipes, the animal should be cut into portions, but whole roasted beavers are preferred by many cooks. In either case, soaking for at least 24 hours in salt water with about ¼ cup of vinegar will be beneficial.

MUSKRAT

Many older hunters have had plenty of experience skinning muskrats, since at one time trapping these animals was the main source of spending money for farm youths. Probably a lot of them also had the pleasure of eating muskrats, the meat of which is similar in texture and taste to that of squirrels, except a bit darker.

For the uninitiated, skinning is an easy process, especially if you aren't trying to keep the hide, and the method of slitting the skin across the back and stripping off the hide is as good as any.

Take care to remove the scent glands, which are much like those on raccoons, except there are also some on the lower part of the belly. Once these are out of the way, cut the meat into pieces, which generally amounts to six: the four legs, loin and rib cage. Then soak in a mild salt and vinegar solution that helps tenderize the meat and draw out any remaining blood from the meat.

SELECTED RECIPES

Cooking and eating game doubles the pleasure of the hunt and provides enjoyment for those who get to share in the bounty. Wild game is much more nutritious than domestic meat, since it is free of chemical and organic additives. There are countless ways to cook wild game and enough different recipes to fill several books. However, here are a few traditional favorites:

Southern Squirrel 'n Dumplings

2 squirrels, cut in serving pieces
2 bay leaves
1 cup onions, sliced
1 cup chopped celery
8 carrots, split and halved
1 tsp. salt
½ tsp. pepper
Dumplings:
2 cups flour
½ tsp. salt
4 tsp. baking powder
¾ cup milk

Cover squirrel with 1 inch of water, add bay leaves and simmer for 1¼ hours. Skim fat, then add onions, celery, carrots, salt and pepper. Add 1½ cups water and cook for 15 minutes. Prepare dumplings: sift dry ingredients, then add milk gradually. Roll on floured board until ½ inch thick. Cut into 3-inch squares and add to kettle contents. Cover and cook 15 minutes. Serves 4.

Batter-Fried Squirrel

2 squirrels, cut in serving pieces
4 cups boiling water
1 onion, chopped
1 carrot, sliced
1 stalk celery, diced
1 sprig fresh parsley, chopped
Batter:
½ cup flour
½ cup cornmeal
1 tsp. baking powder
¼ tsp. salt
1 egg, lightly beaten
¾ cup milk

Drop squirrel pieces into boiling water, add onion, carrot, celery and parsley. Simmer until squirrel is tender. Pour off liquid and reserve for gravy. Refrigerate meat until cool. While meat is cooling, prepare batter: mix dry ingredients, combine milk with beaten egg, then add to the flour mixture. Dry the meat, then dip in batter and deep fry until nicely browned. Serve with your favorite cream-style gravy. Serves 4.

Squirrel Stew Diablo

3 squirrels
2 onions, chopped
1 green pepper, chopped
1 Jalapeno pepper, chopped
3 medium potatoes, diced
¼ cup diced celery
4 Tbsp. chili powder
Salt and pepper to taste
Dash Louisiana hot sauce
1½ cups cooked rice

Cook squirrels in water to cover until tender. Remove from water and refrigerate to cool, reserving broth. Remove meat from the bones and add to broth. Add onions, peppers, potatoes, celery and spices. Cook for 45 minutes. Serve hot over cooked rice. Serves 6.

Barbecued Rabbit

3 lbs. rabbit, cut in serving pieces
Flour, salt and pepper
Your favorite barbecue sauce
¼ cup cooking oil

Preheat oven to 325 degrees. Coat rabbit pieces in mixture of flour, salt and pepper. Heat oil in an oven-ready skillet. Add rabbit and brown on all sides over moderate heat. Pour barbecue sauce into pan and cover. Bake for 45 minutes, then uncover and brown under broiler for 10 to 15 minutes. Serves 6.

Braised Rabbit

5-lb. rabbit, split
Salt and pepper to taste
2 Tbsp. vegetable oil
1 cup consomme
2 sprigs fresh thyme
1 carrot, diced
½ onion, chopped

Preheat oven to 400 degrees. Heat oil in a heavy skillet. Add rabbit, sprinkle with salt and pepper, and brown on all sides. Meanwhile heat consomme with thyme for 5 minutes. Strain, then reheat and add carrot and onion. Put rabbit pieces into baking pan. Pour consomme mixture over rabbit. Cover and bake for 45 minutes, basting occasionally. Serves 4–6.

Stewed Rabbit in Juice

2 rabbits, cut in serving pieces
¼ cup vegetable oil
2 large onions, diced
2 cloves minced garlic
½ cup celery, diced
8 oz. mushrooms, sliced
2 Tbsp. flour
½ cup water
½ cup pear juice
½ cup pineapple juice
1 tsp. salt
½ tsp. pepper
¼ tsp. thyme

Brown rabbit in vegetable oil in a large skillet or Dutch oven. Remove meat. Saute onions, garlic, celery and mushrooms until tender. Add flour. Combine water, pear and pineapple juice and add gradually. Season with salt, pepper and thyme. Bring to a boil and simmer for five minutes. Add rabbit meat, cover, and simmer for 30 to 40 minutes until tender. Serves 4–6.

Raccoon and Sweet Potatoes

1 raccoon
Vinegar
Water to cover
Salt and pepper to taste
Cayenne pepper to taste
2 cloves minced garlic
1 cup celery, diced
1 large onion, chopped
1 green pepper, chopped
Vegetable oil
Flour
4 medium sweet potatoes

Soak raccoon for one hour in a vinegar/water solution. Drain. Cut into serving pieces and place in a pan with water to cover. Add salt, pepper, cayenne, garlic, celery, onion and green pepper. Boil until partially tender. Remove meat. Heat a small amount of vegetable oil in a skillet. Add raccoon and brown on all sides. Remove. Make a thin gravy with flour and drippings. Place meat in roasting pan; add gravy. Bake at 350 degrees for 30 minutes. Peel and halve sweet potatoes. Place around meat in roasting pan. Continue baking until potatoes are done. Serves 4.

Roast Raccoon 'n Dressing

1 raccoon
Water to cover
Vinegar
1 tsp. baking soda
Salt and pepper
Dressing:
3 cups dry bread crumbs
2 Tbsp. melted butter
1 small onion, chopped
1 cooking apple thinly sliced
½ tsp. salt
¼ tsp. pepper

Preheat oven to 375 degrees. Parboil raccoon for 30 minutes in water and baking soda. Meanwhile, prepare dressing: combine bread crumbs, butter, onion, apple, salt and pepper; add water until moist. Drain meat. Rub inside and out with salt and pepper. Stuff with dressing; place in roasting pan and bake for 1½ hours or until tender and nicely browned, skimming fat as it accumulates and adding water. Before serving, rub meat with a cloth soaked in vinegar. Serves 4.

Raccoon, Curry Style

2 young raccoons
Salted water to cover
1 med. onion, quartered
¼ tsp. Tabasco sauce
3 medium onions, chopped fine
1 Tbsp. paprika
1 bay leaf
1 piece stick cinnamon
3 Tbsp. butter
4 Tbsp. curry powder
2 cups chicken stock
2 tomatoes, diced
1 tsp. salt
1 lemon, thinly sliced
1 cup sour cream

Heat salted water, onion and Tabasco sauce. Add raccoon and parboil for 30 minutes. Cool meat, remove from bones, and cut in 1-inch cubes. Brown butter in large skillet; add curry powder and meat. Stir over heat until mixture is dark. Add stock, tomatoes, onions, seasonings and lemon. Simmer until meat is tender. Reduce heat; add sour cream. Remove when heated through but not boiling. Serves 4–6.

Roast Stuffed Opossum

1 opossum
Salt and pepper
1 quart water
Dressing
1 Tbsp. vegetable oil
1 onion, chopped
Opossum liver

1 cup bread crumbs
¼ tsp. Worcestershire sauce
1 hard-boiled egg, chopped
1 tsp. salt

Preheat oven to 350 degrees. Wash the cleaned opossum in soda water. Rub inside and out with salt and pepper. Prepare dressing: saute onion in oil. Add opossum liver and cook until tender; chop liver. Remove from heat. Mix bread crumbs, Worcestershire sauce, egg and salt, adding water to moisten. Add liver and onions. Stuff opossum with dressing; truss. Place on rack in roasting pan and add 1 qt. water. Roast 2½ hours or until tender, basting every 15 minutes. Serves 4–6.

Granny's Opossum and Yams

1 opossum
Salt and pepper to taste
Flour
½ cup water
4 medium yams
¼ tsp. salt
2 Tbsp. brown sugar

Preheat oven to 350 degrees. Rub salt/pepper mixture over opossum inside and out. Coat inside and out with flour. Place the opossum on its back in a roasting pan; add water. Cover and bake for 45 minutes. Peel yams, split lengthwise, and place in pan around edge. Add water if needed. Continue baking for 30 minutes; remove cover. Sprinkle yams with salt and brown sugar. Bake uncovered until meat and yams are brown and tender. Serves 4.

Apple-Roasted Opossum

1 young opossum
Stuffing (your recipe)
Bacon strips
3 cups water
1 Tbsp. sugar
1 Tbsp. lemon juice
6 apples, pared and quartered

1 cup brown sugar

1 tsp. lemon rind

1 tsp. ground cinnamon

Preheat oven to 350 degrees. Stuff cleaned opossum; place on rack in roaster and cover with bacon. Add sugar and lemon juice to water; pour into bottom of roaster. Bake for 2 hours. Drain all but 1 cup of liquid from pan. Surround opossum with apples. Mix the brown sugar, lemon rind and cinnamon; sprinkle on apples. Continue roasting for 30 minutes or until meat is tender. Serves 4.

Woodchuck Italiano

1 woodchuck

8 cups water

½ cup salt

4 mint leaves

¼ cup olive oil

1 clove minced garlic

Salt and pepper to taste

½ cup vinegar

2 cups tomato sauce

1 tsp. basil

Soak dressed chuck overnight in cold water and salt. Remove, cut in 8 pieces and boil 15 minutes in clear water. Rinse meat, return to salt water and repeat soaking process. Rinse again; boil in clear water with mint leaves for 45 minutes. Drain. Salt and pepper both sides and brown in skillet with oil and garlic. Add vinegar; cover and simmer 8 minutes. Remove to cooking pot. Add tomato sauce and basil. Cook over moderate heat for 1½ hours. Serves 4–6.

Woodchuck Burgers

Ground meat of 1 woodchuck

½ cup fresh bread crumbs

½ cup onion, diced

1 tsp. salt

¼ tsp. pepper

2 eggs

1 Tbsp. melted butter

White cornmeal

3 Tbsp. vegetable oil

1 cup catsup

½ tsp. Worcestershire sauce

Preheat oven to 325 degrees. Beat one egg. Combine ground meat, bread crumbs, onion, salt, pepper, egg and butter. Mix well and shape into 8 patties. Beat remaining egg. Dip patties into egg, then coat with cornmeal. Fry until brown in hot oil. Mix catsup and Worcestershire sauce and pour over patties. Bake for 1 hour. Serves 8.

Woodchuck in Sour Cream Sauce

1 woodchuck, cut in serving pieces

Water to cover

1 small onion, sliced

1 tsp. salt

4 laurel leaves

6 whole allspice

¼ cup vinegar

1 Tbsp. flour

1½ cups sour cream

Put chuck pieces in deep pan; cover with water. Add onions, seasonings and vinegar. Simmer until meat is tender. Remove meat, strain stock and return to pan. Mix flour and sour cream; add to simmering stock. Add meat; heat thoroughly but do not allow to boil. Serves 4–6.

Roast Beaver

1 beaver

Water to cover

¼ cup vinegar

Salt and pepper

¼ lb. salt pork, cut in strips

⅓ cup diced onion

⅓ cup diced carrot

⅓ cup diced celery

Flour

Remove all surface fat from beaver; soak overnight in water mixed with vinegar. Preheat oven to 350 degrees. Remove meat; rinse; place on rack in roaster. Cut several slits in meat and rub with salt and pepper; cover slits with salt pork and dust with a little flour. Add ½ cup water to pan; cover. Roast for 30 minutes. Add more water if needed. Sprinkle diced vegetables over meat. Continue roasting uncovered until meat falls off the bones. Use pan juices for gravy. Serves 4–6.

Onion-Fried Beaver

1 beaver
Salted water to cover
3 bay leaves
4 cloves
2 onions, sliced
2 Tbsp. butter
Vegetable oil
Flour
Salt and pepper to taste

Soak dressed beaver overnight in salted water; cut into serving pieces. Add bay leaves and cloves to clear water and parboil meat for 30 minutes. Meanwhile, saute onion slices in butter and 2 tablespoons vegetable oil until translucent. Remove onions to another container. Add salt and pepper to flour. Dry meat pieces and roll in seasoned flour mixture. Fry in butter and oil until meat is brown. Top with saute ed onions. Serves 6.

Beaver Tail *Henri*

1 beaver tail
1 cup red wine
1 cup water
1 large onion, chopped
½ cup vinegar
1 tsp. salt
Flour
1 beaten egg
1 cup cracker crumbs
3 Tbsp. melted butter
1 lemon, thinly sliced

Marinate beaver tail for 24 hours in mixture

of red wine, water, and onion. Preheat oven to 350 degrees. Dry tail and scrape carefully. Add vinegar and salt to enough water to cover the meat. Parboil until nearly tender. Dry tail again; coat lightly with flour. Dip meat into beaten egg, then into cracker crumbs. Place on rack in roasting pan; drizzle butter over meat. Roast until tender and nicely browned. Garnish with lemon slices before serving. Serves 2.

Fried Muskrat with Milk Gravy

2 muskrats, quartered
Water to cover
Salt
2 eggs, beaten
½ cup milk
Flour
White cornmeal
Vegetable oil
3 Tbsp. flour
1½ cups milk

Soak muskrat pieces for 1 hour in salted water. Rinse and pat dry; sprinkle with salt and pepper. Blend beaten eggs with ½ cup milk. Dip meat in flour, then in egg mixture, then in cornmeal. Brown on all sides in hot oil, then lower heat and simmer 1 hour. Remove meat; pour off oil, returning 3 tablespoons to skillet. Add remaining ingredients to make milk gravy; cook until thickened. Serves 2.

Barbecued Muskrat

4 muskrats
2 qt. water
2 cups vinegar
¼ cup salt
Vegetable oil
Barbecue Sauce:
½ cup butter
1 large onion, grated
½ cup water
1 Tbsp. Worcestershire sauce
3 Tbsp. lemon juice

1 tsp. salt

½ tsp. pepper

2 tsp. paprika

½ tsp. dry mustard

1 Tbsp. brown sugar

2 Tbsp. tomato paste

Soak muskrat in water, vinegar and salt for up to 24 hours. Preheat oven to 350 degrees. Meanwhile, prepare barbecue sauce: saute onion in butter until it is translucent. Add remaining ingredients and simmer for 10 minutes. Drain muskrat and pat dry; cut in serving pieces. Brown on all side in hot oil. Place in baking dish and cover with barbecue sauce; bake for 1 hour, basting frequently with sauce. Serves 4.

There's the standing joke about "eating crow," but there is a recipe that puts a different slant on the saying.

"Eat Crow" Casserole

6 crows

Salted water to cover

2 cans mushroom soup

2 cups cooked rice

Soak birds overnight in salt water. Rinse; simmer in clear water until tender; drain. Preheat oven to 350 degrees. Remove meat from bones. Heat soup in saucepan. Add half of the meat. Spread half of the rice in a casserole; add remaining meat. Form a second layer with the remaining rice; pour soup and meat mixture over all. Cover dish and bake for 15 minutes. Serves 6.

PHOTO CREDITS

All photos by Aubrey Watson unless otherwise credited